Color The world: Coloring Book

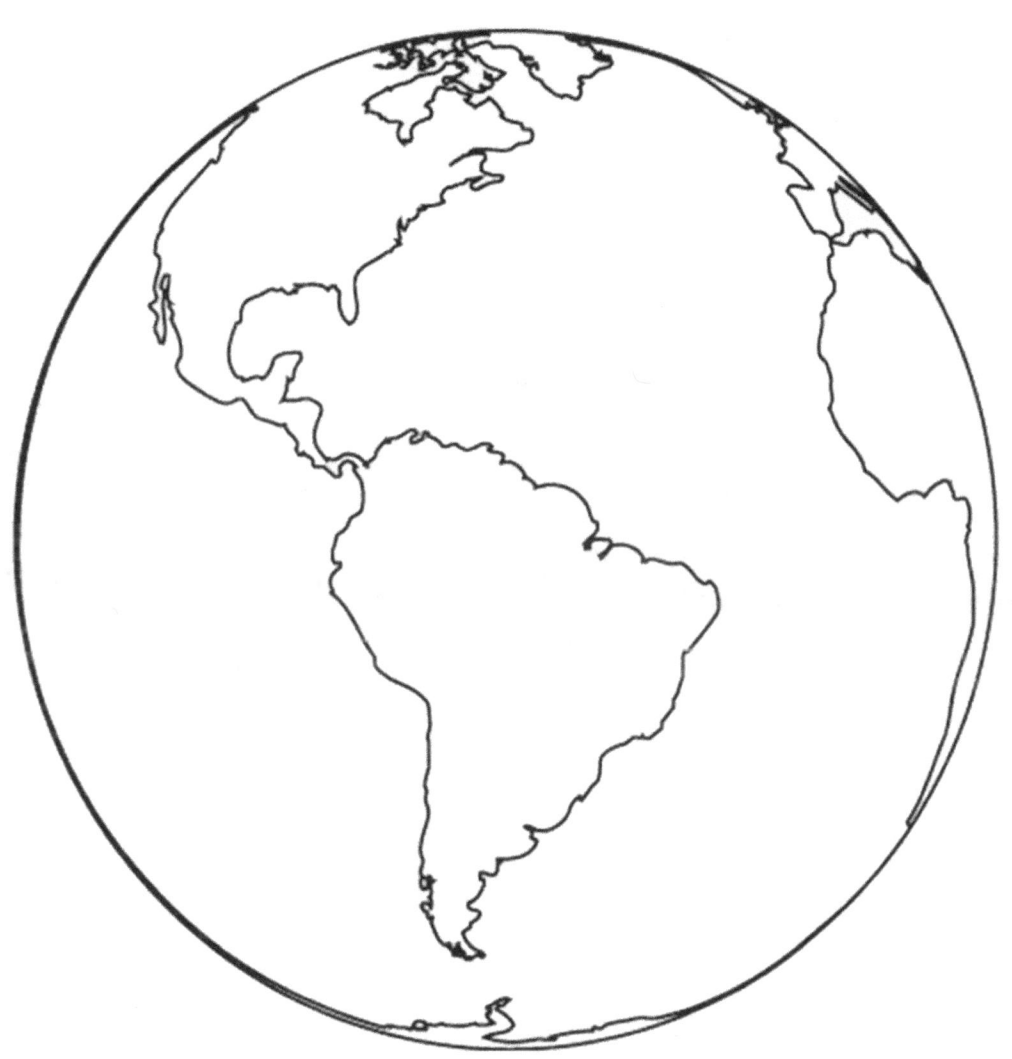

Nina Watson

Color The world

Copyright: Published in the United States by **Nina Watson**
Published November 2017

All rights reserved. No part of this publication may be reproduced, stored in retrieval system, copied in any form or by any means, electronic, mechanical, photocopying, recording or otherwise transmitted without written permission from the publisher. Please do not participate in or encourage piracy of this material in any way. You must not circulate this book in any format Nina Watson does not control or direct users' actions and is not responsible for the information or content shared, harm and/or actions of the book readers.

ISBN-13: 978-1979751865

ISBN-10: 1979751862

Big Ben is the nickname for the Great Bell of the clock at the north end of the Palace of Westminster in London

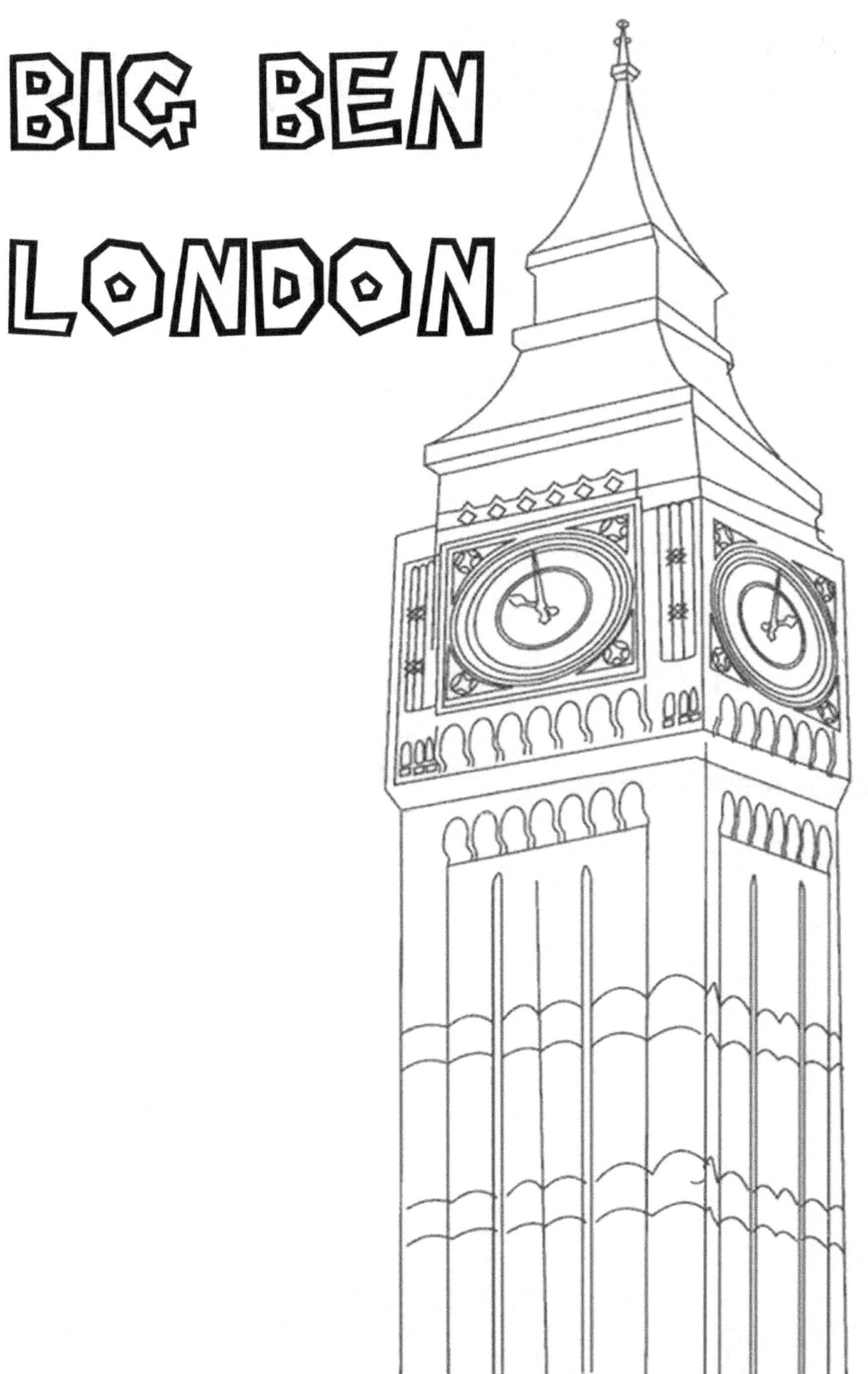

London Bridge have spanned the River Thames between the City of London and Southwark, in central London.

LONDON BRIDGE

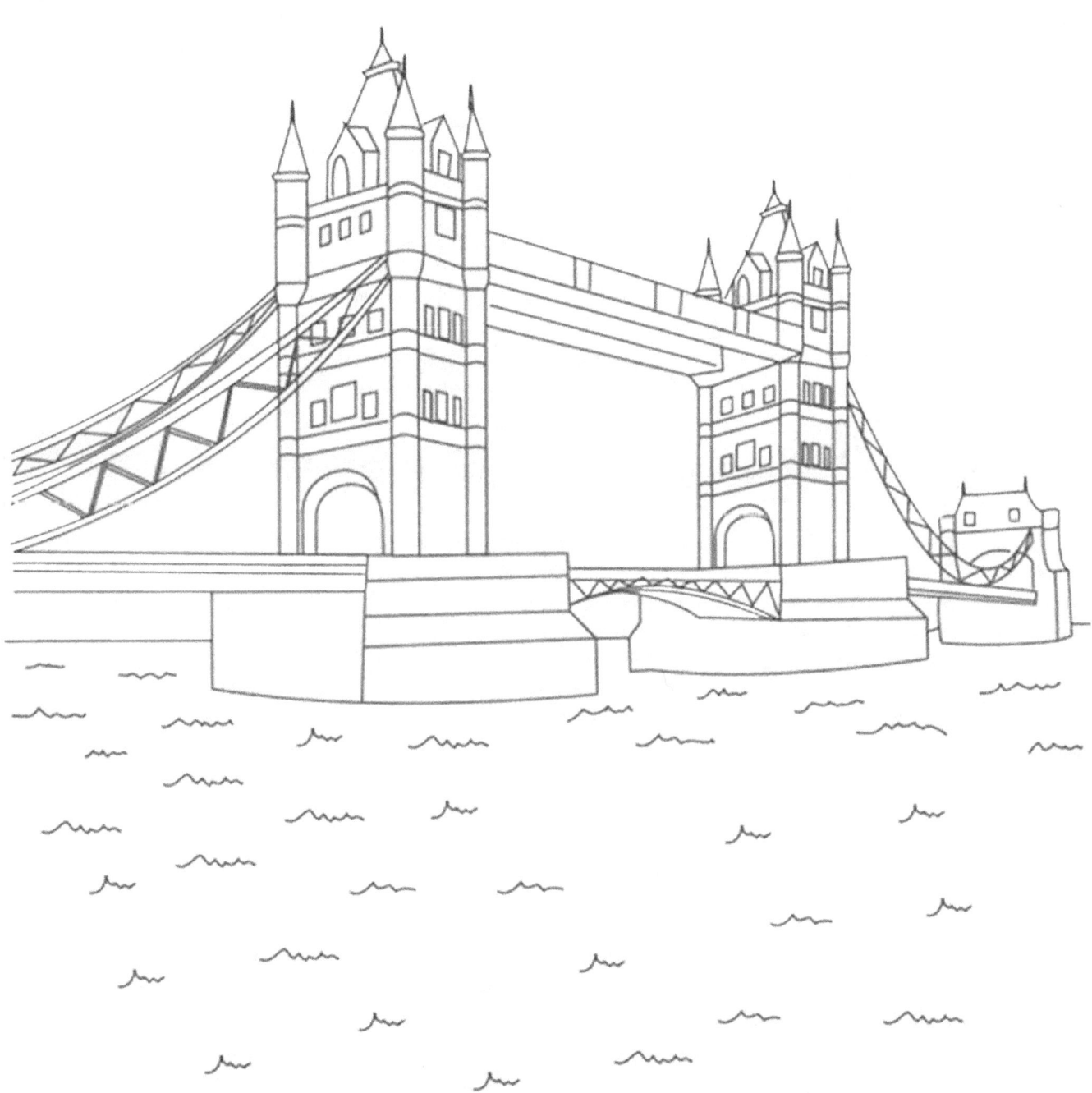

Stonehenge is a prehistoric monument in Wiltshire, England

STONEHENGE

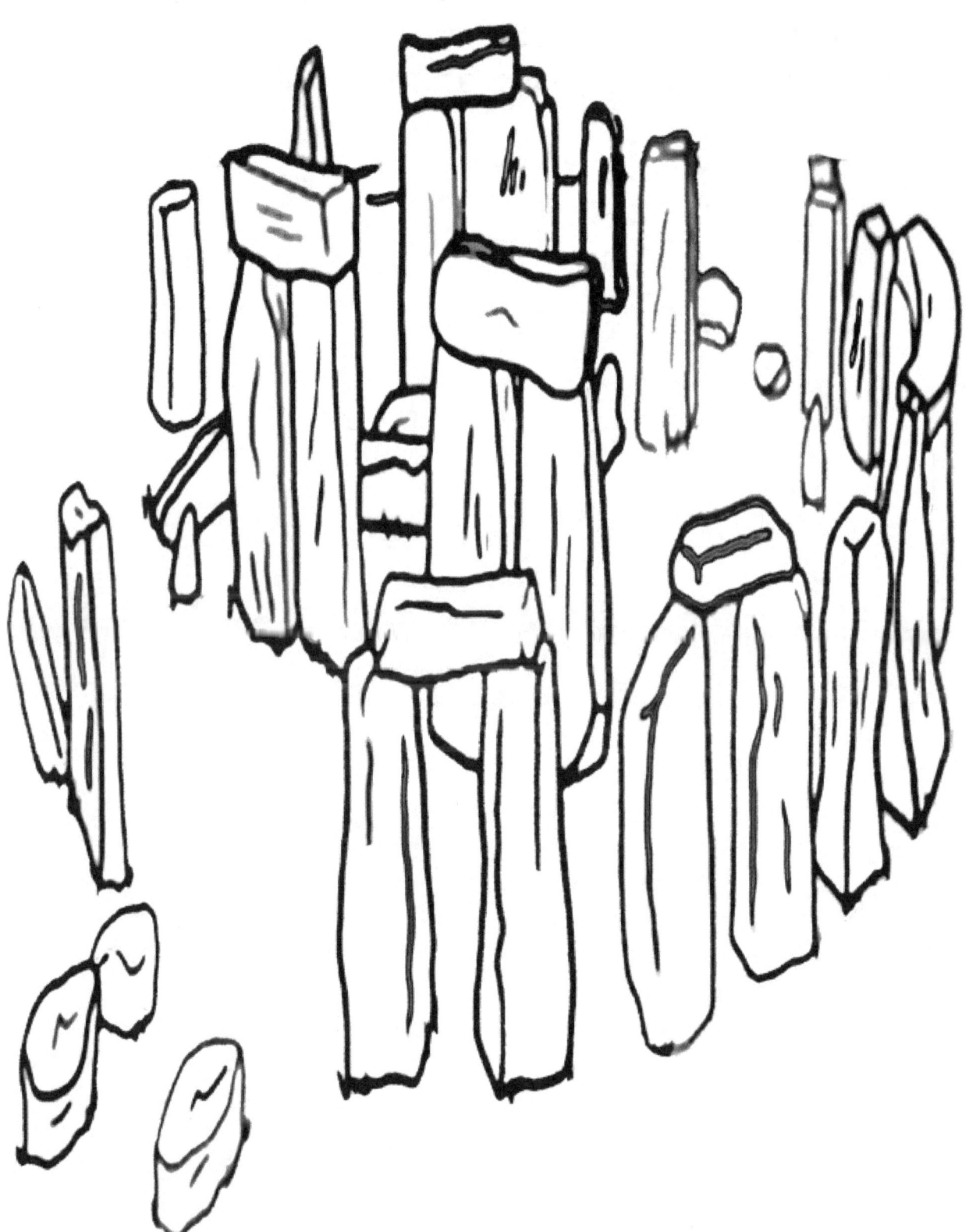

The Colosseum or Flavian Amphitheatre is a large ellipsoid arena built in the first century CE under the Roman emperors of the Flavian dynasty. The arena was used to host spectacular public entertainment events such as gladiator fights, wild animal hunts and public executions

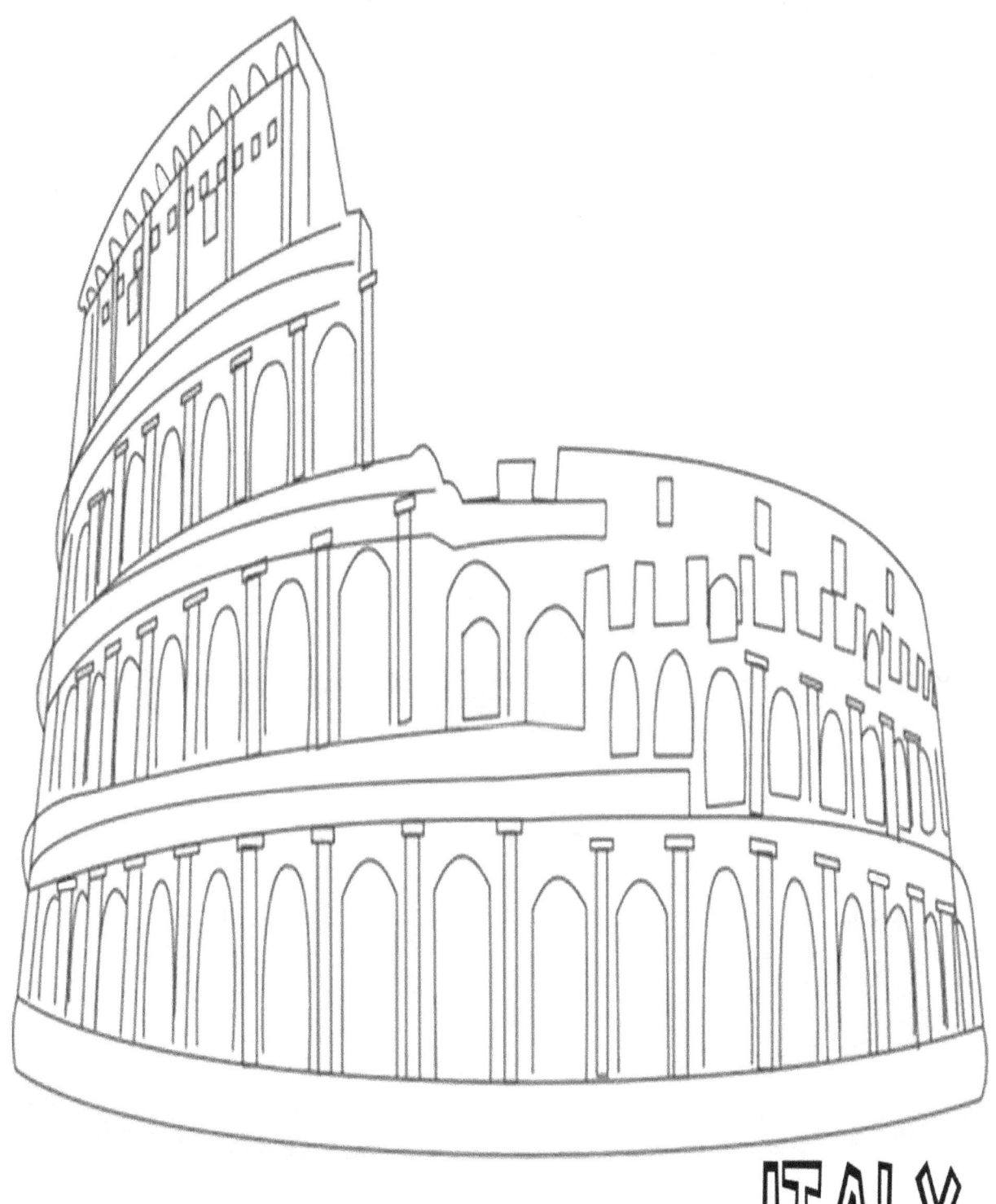

The Leaning Tower of is the campanile, or freestanding bell tower, of the cathedral of the Italian city of Pisa

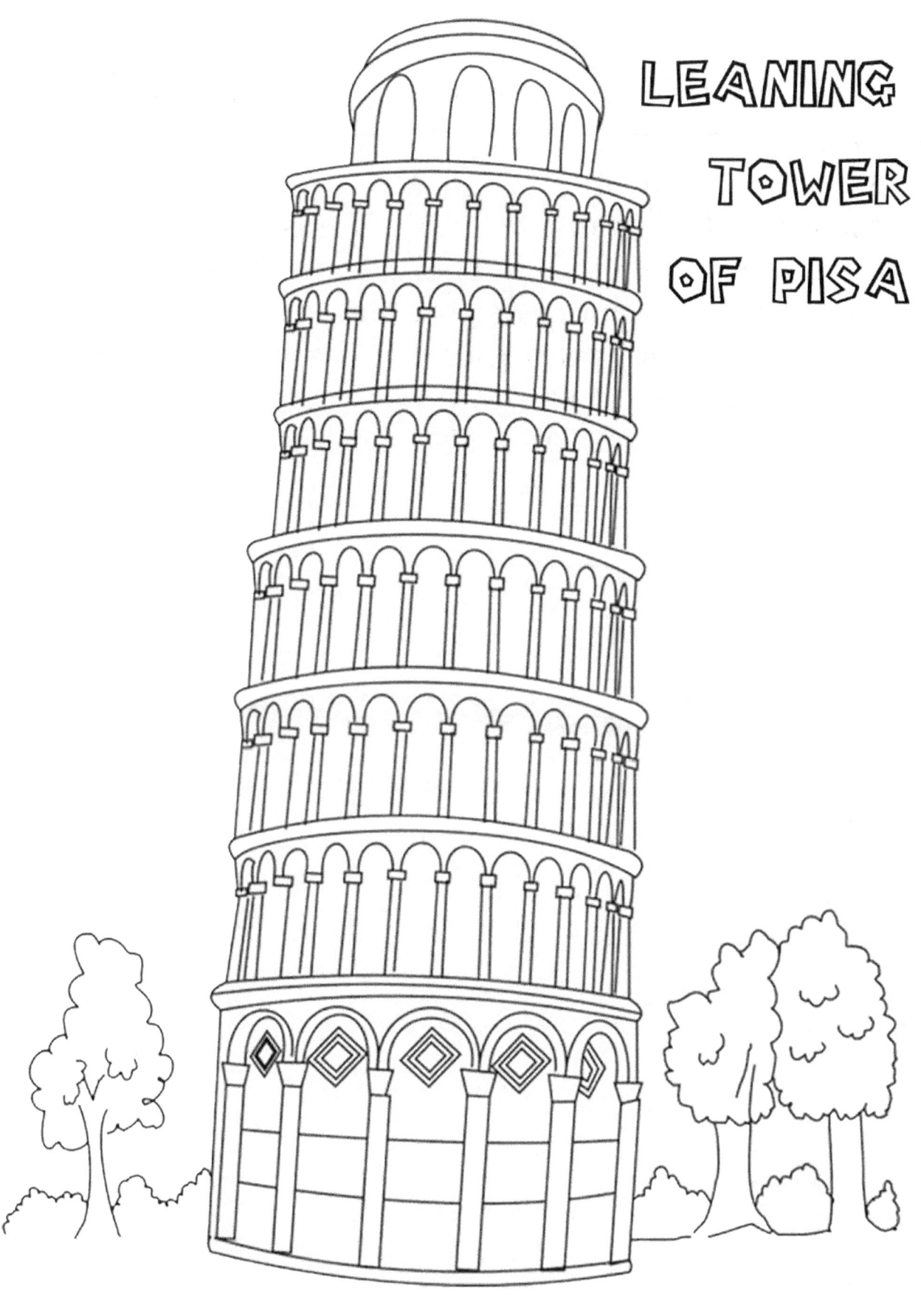

Venice is a city in northeastern Italy and the capital of the Veneto region. It is situated across a group of 118 small islands that are separated by canals and linked by bridges, of which there are 400. The islands are located in the shallow Venetian Lagoon, an enclosed bay that lies between the mouths of the Po and the Piave Rivers. Parts of Venice are renowned for the beauty of their settings, their architecture, and artwork. The lagoon and a part of the city are listed as a World Heritage Site.

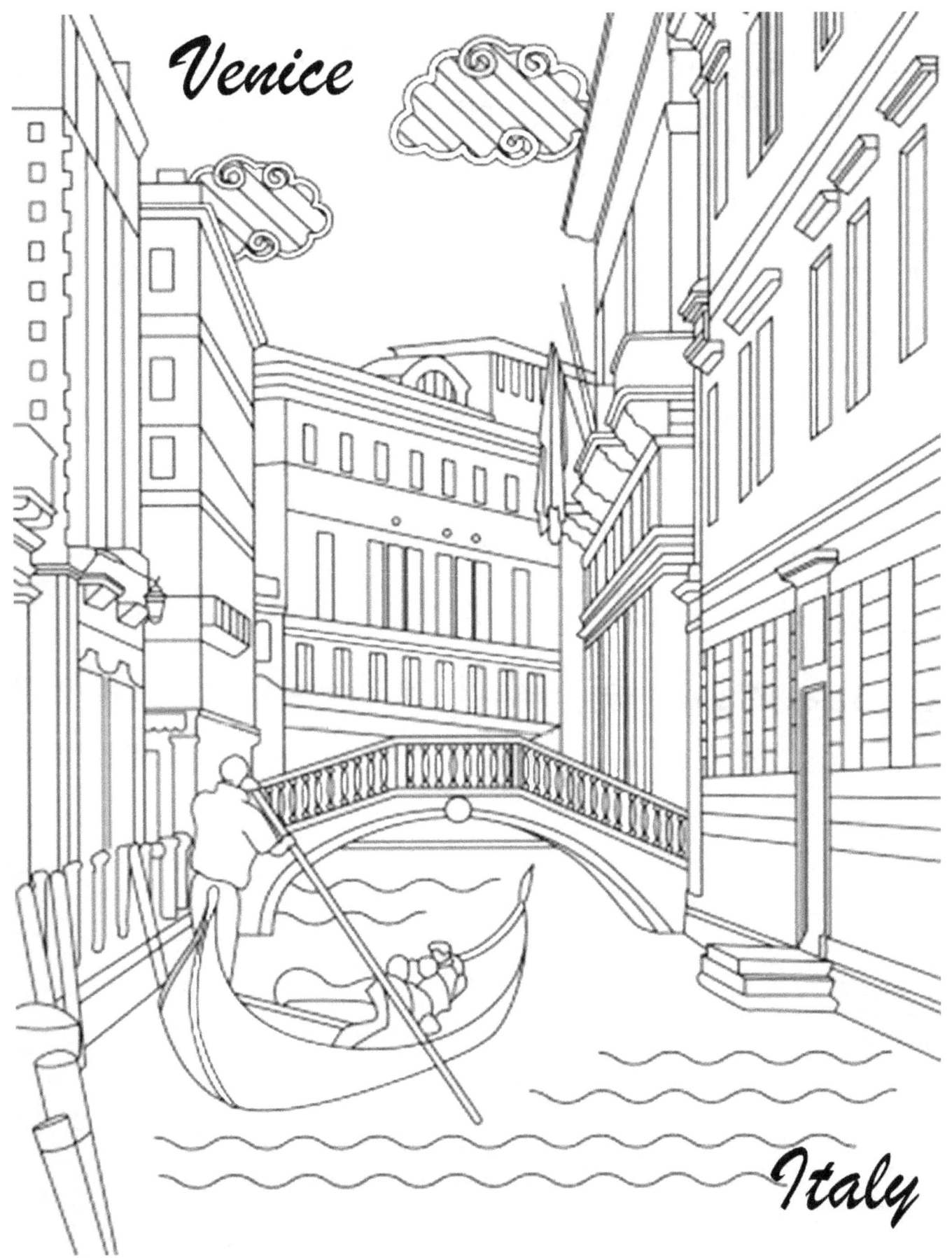

The Eiffel Tower is a wrought iron lattice tower on the Champ de Mars in Paris, France.

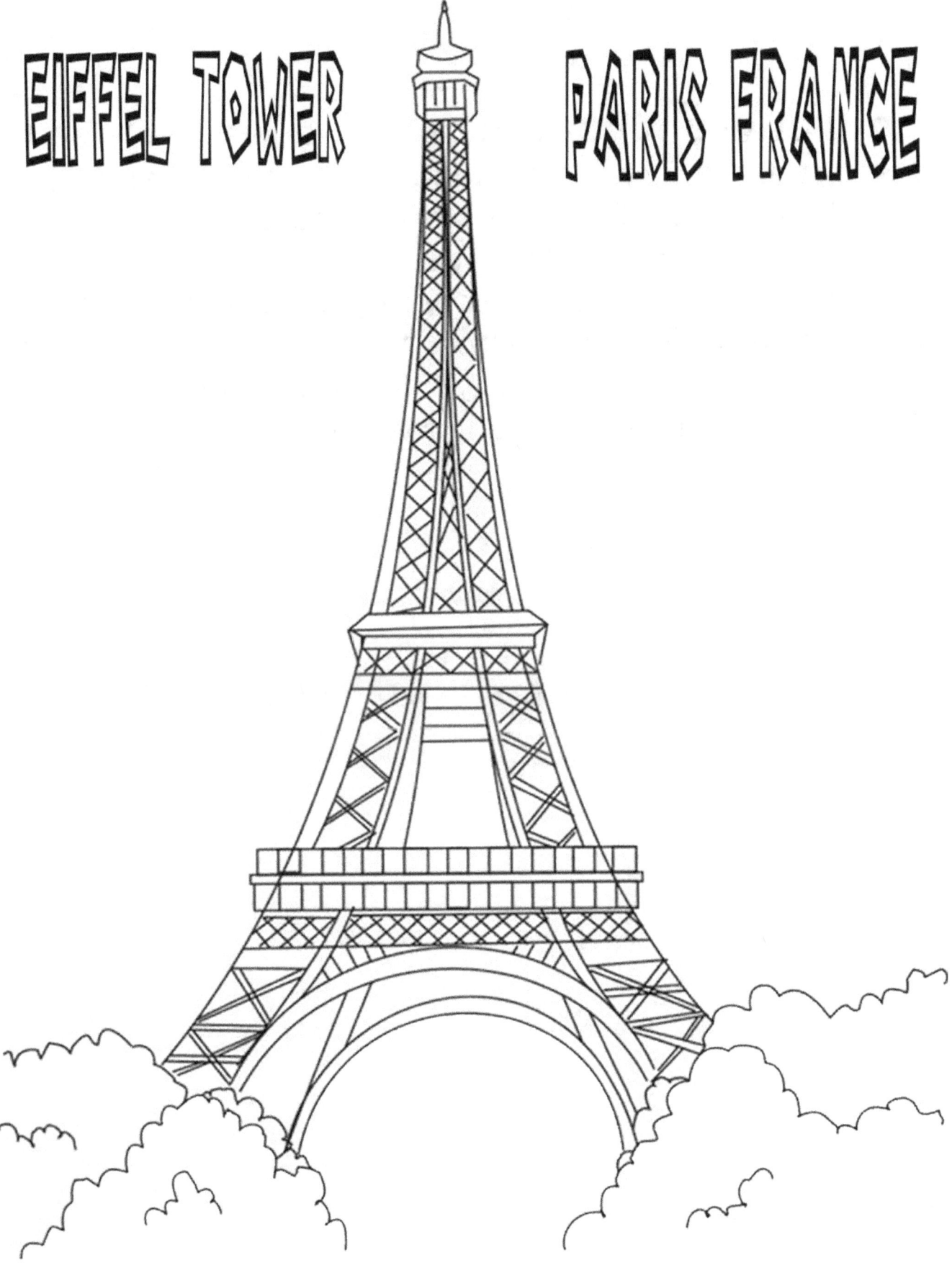

The **Louvre Museum** is the world's largest art museum and a historic monument in Paris, France. A central landmark of the city, it is located on the Right Bank of the Seine in the city's 1st arrondissement (district or ward). Approximately 38,000 objects from prehistory to the 21st century are exhibited over an area of 72,735 square metres (782,910 square feet). The Louvre in 2016 was the world's most visited art museum, receiving 7.3 million visitors.

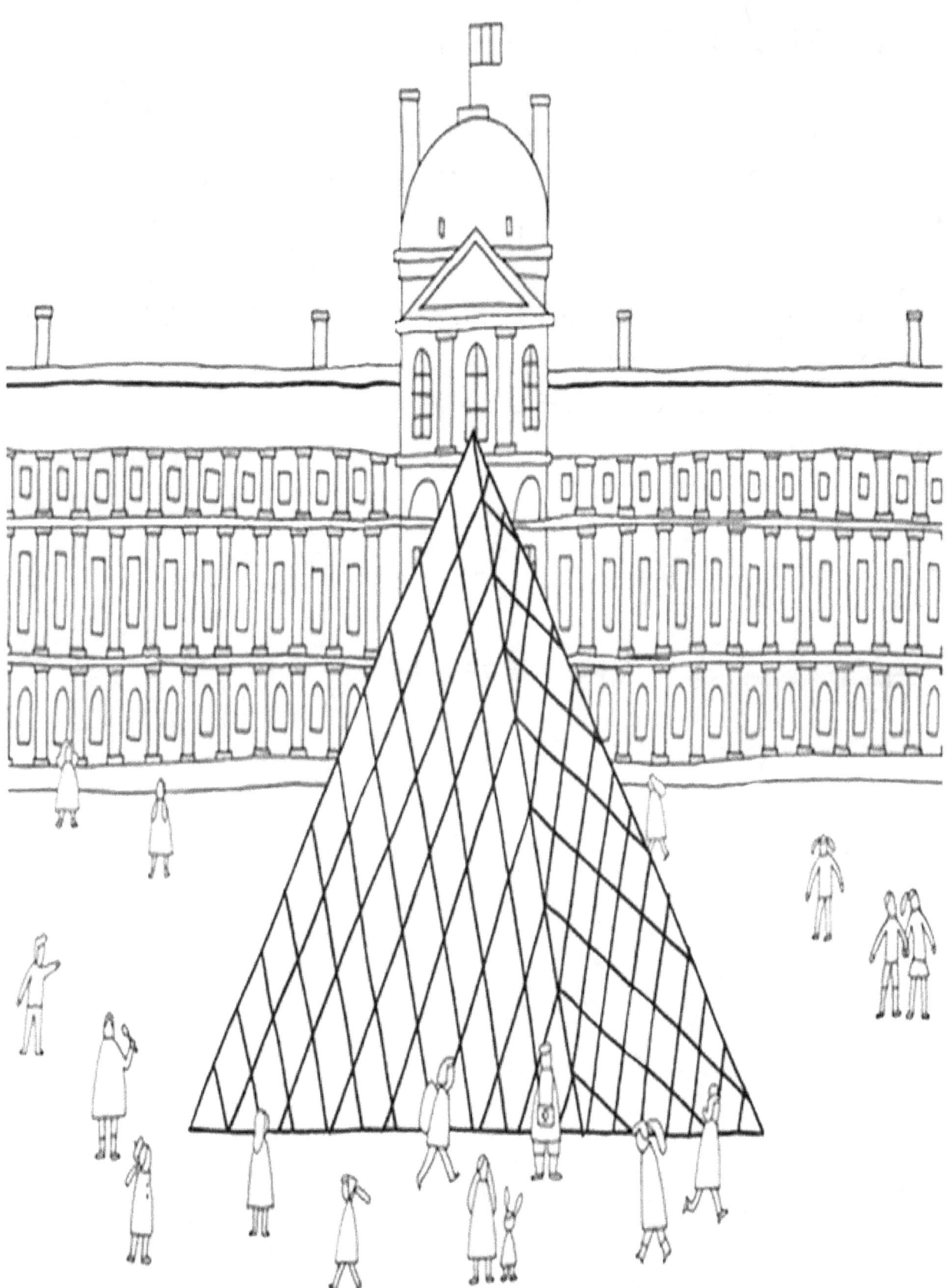

The **Brandenburg Gate** is an 18th-century neoclassical monument in Berlin, built on the orders of Prussian king Frederick William II after the (temporarily) successful restoration of order during the early Batavian Revolution.[1] One of the best-known landmarks of Germany, it was built on the site of a former city gate that marked the start of the road from Berlin to the town of Brandenburg an der Havel, which used to be capital of the Margraviate of Brandenburg.

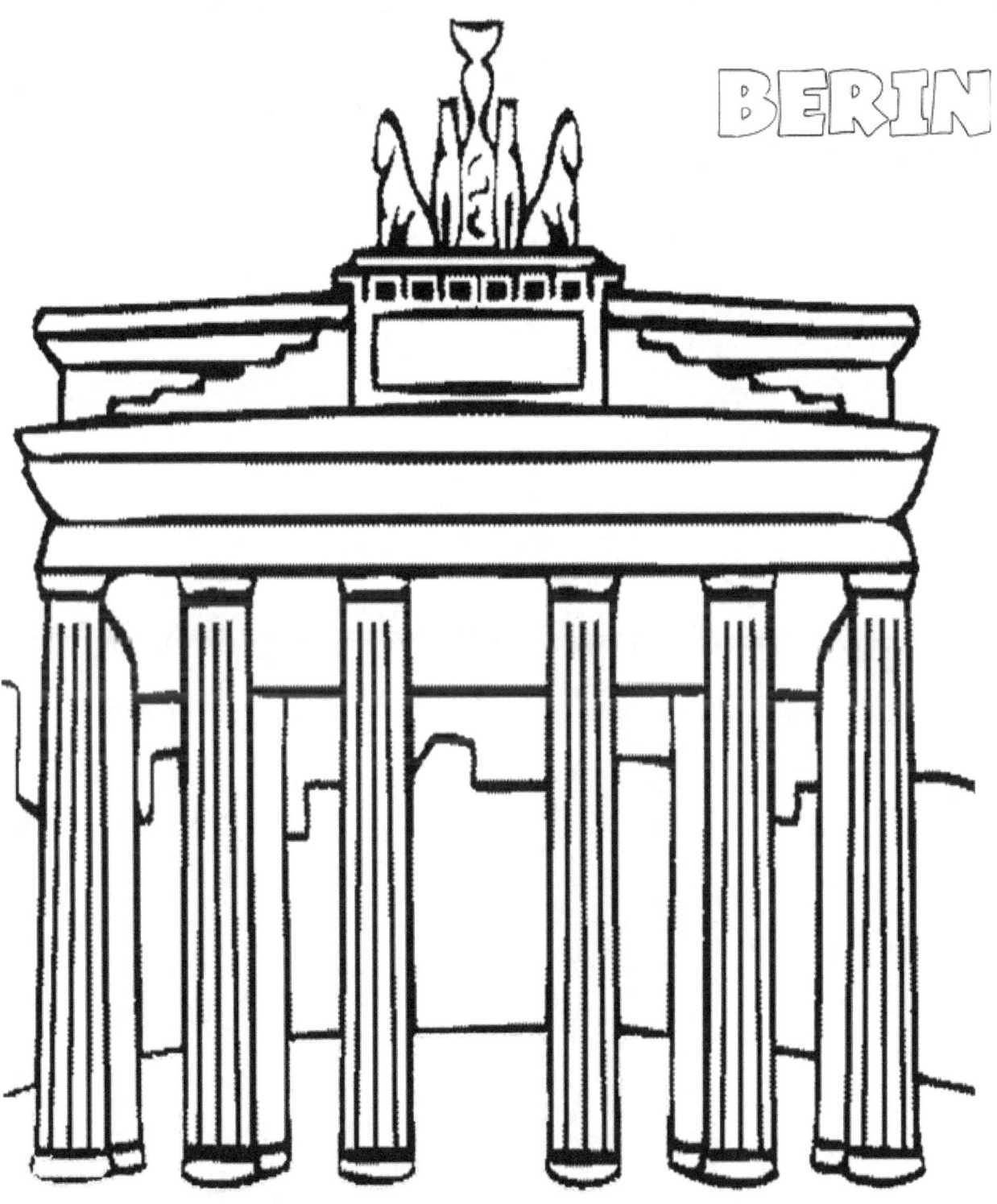

Neuschwanstein Castle is a 19th-century Romanesque Revival palace on a rugged hill above the village of Hohenschwangau near Füssen in southwest Bavaria, Germany.

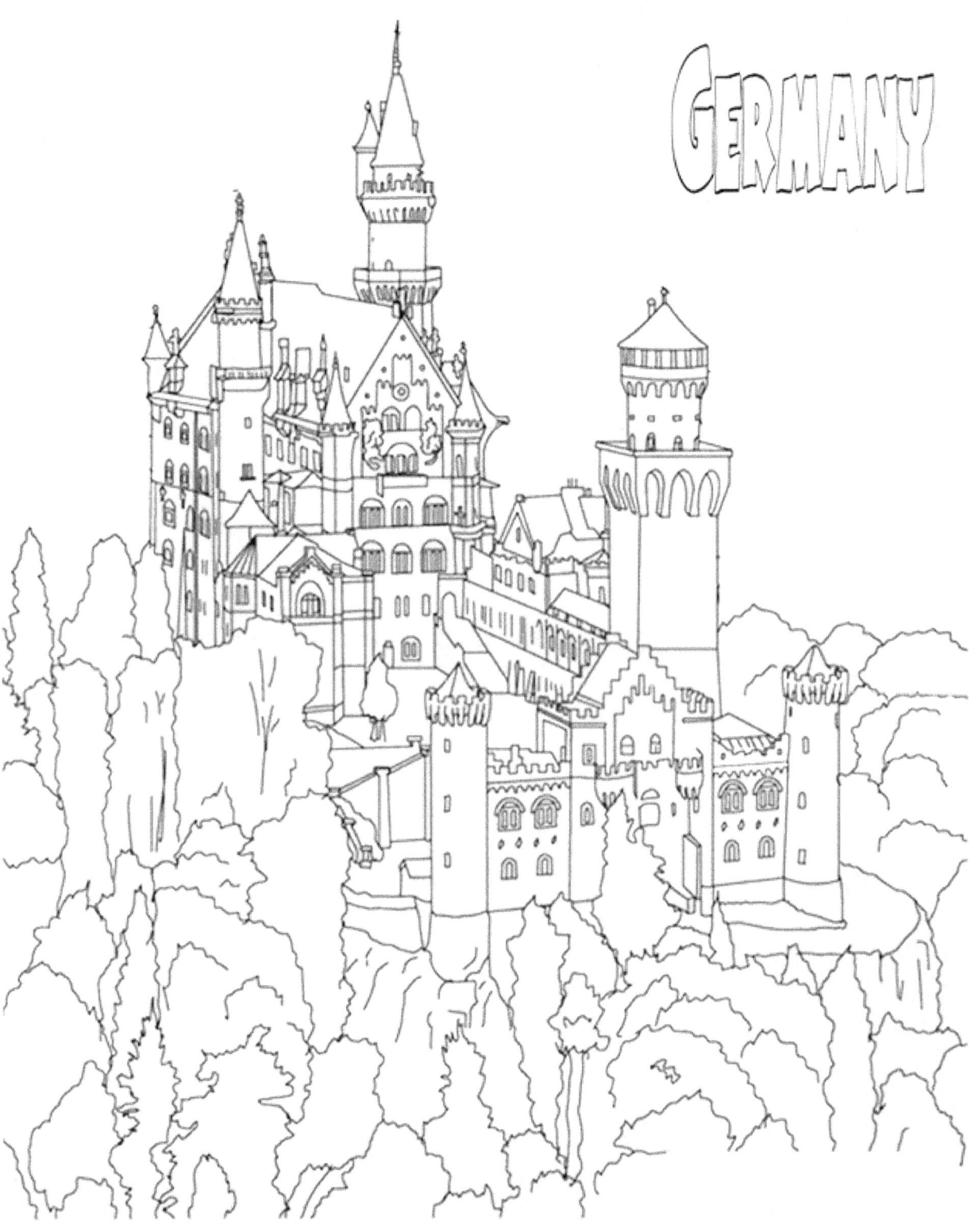

A **windmill** is a mill that converts the energy of wind into rotational energy by means of vanes called sails or blades. Centuries ago, windmills usually were used to mill grain (gristmills), pump water (windpumps), or both. The majority of modern windmills take the form of wind turbines used to generate electricity, or windpumps used to pump water, either for land drainage or to extract groundwater.

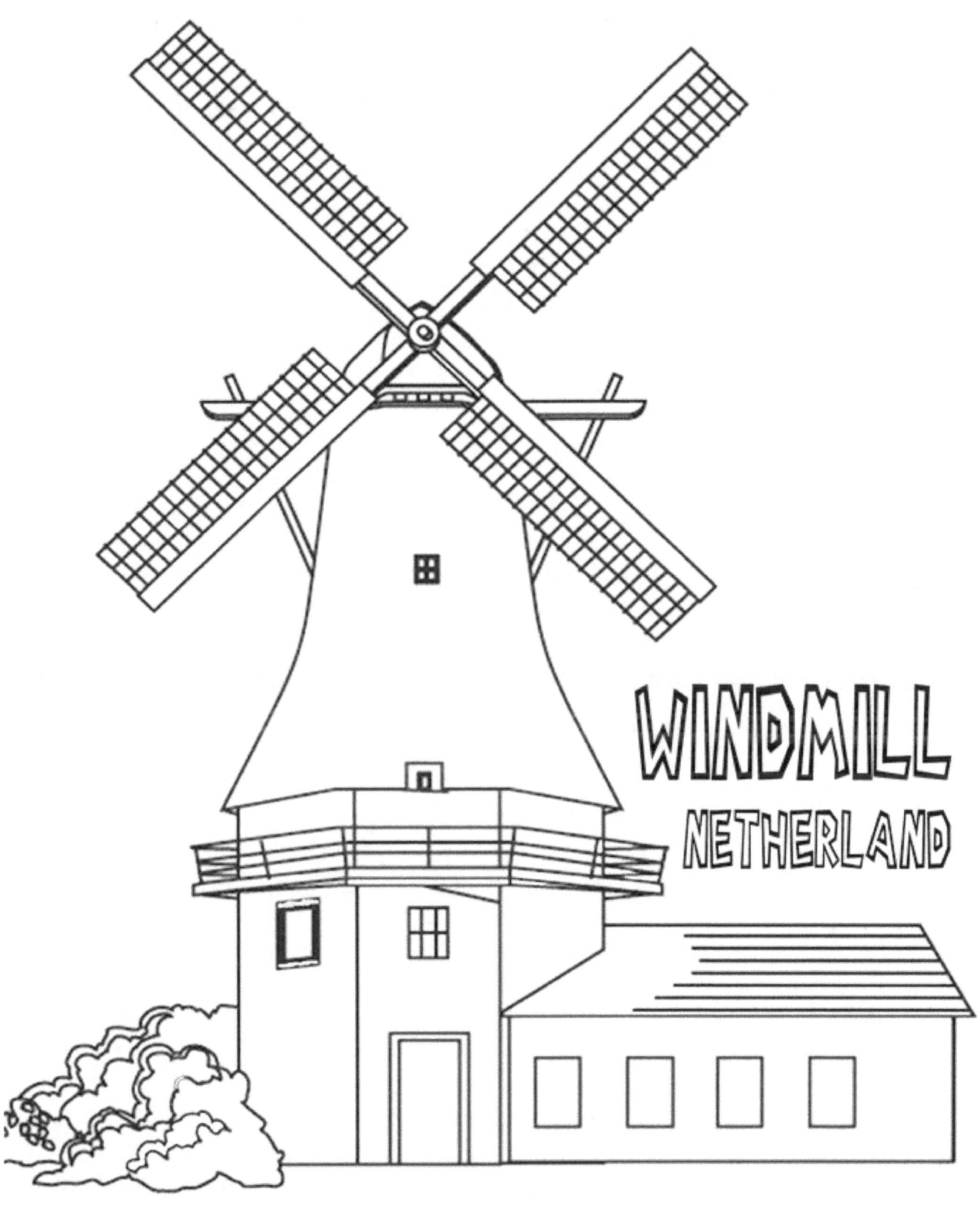

Cristo Rei (Christ the King) is a Catholic monument and shrine located in the city of Almada, across the river Tejo, overlooking the Portuguese capital.

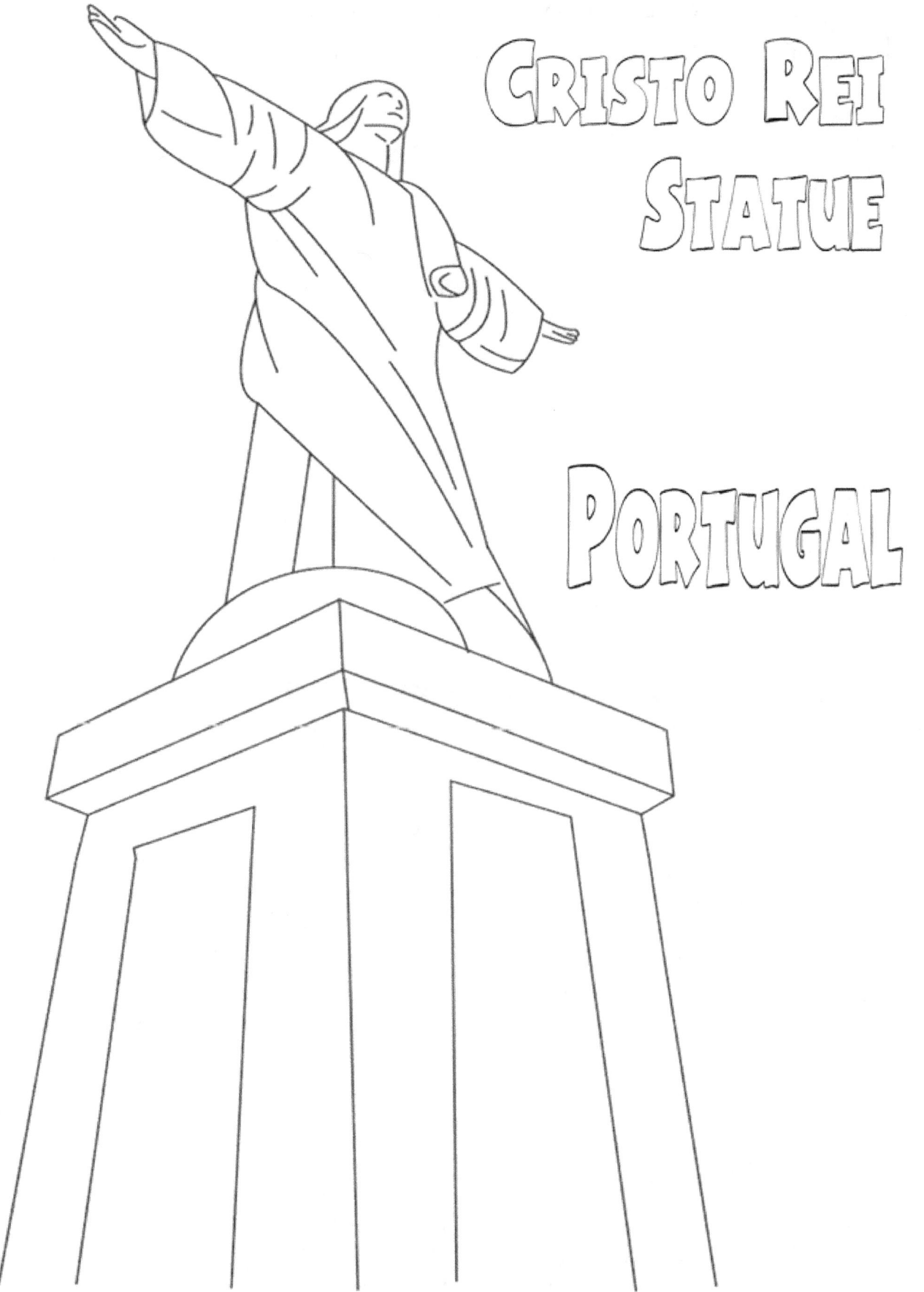

Santorini classically Thera and officially Thira is an island in the southern Aegean Sea

SANTORINI GREECE

The Sultan Ahmed Mosque or Sultan Ahmet Mosque (Turkish: Sultan Ahmet Camii) is a historic mosque located in Istanbul, Turkey.

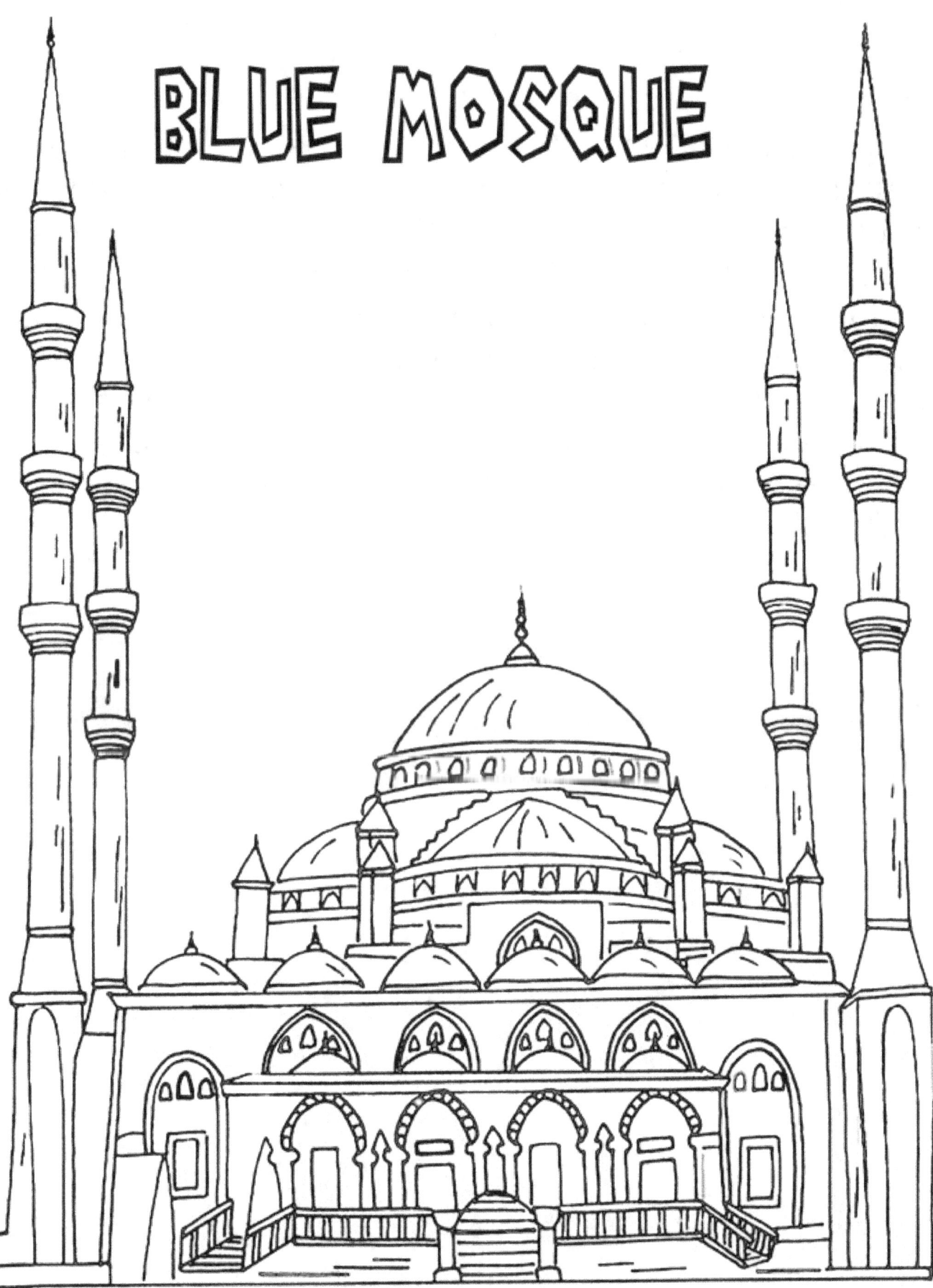

Hagia Sophia is a museum, formerly Greek Orthodox church which was converted into a mosque in 1584, and located in Trabzon, in the north-eastern part of Turkey. It dates back to the thirteenth century when Trabzon was the capital of the Empire of Trebizond. It is located near the seashore and two miles west of the medieval town's limits. It is one of a few dozen Byzantine sites still extant in the area. It has been described as being "regarded as one of the finest examples of Byzantine architecture

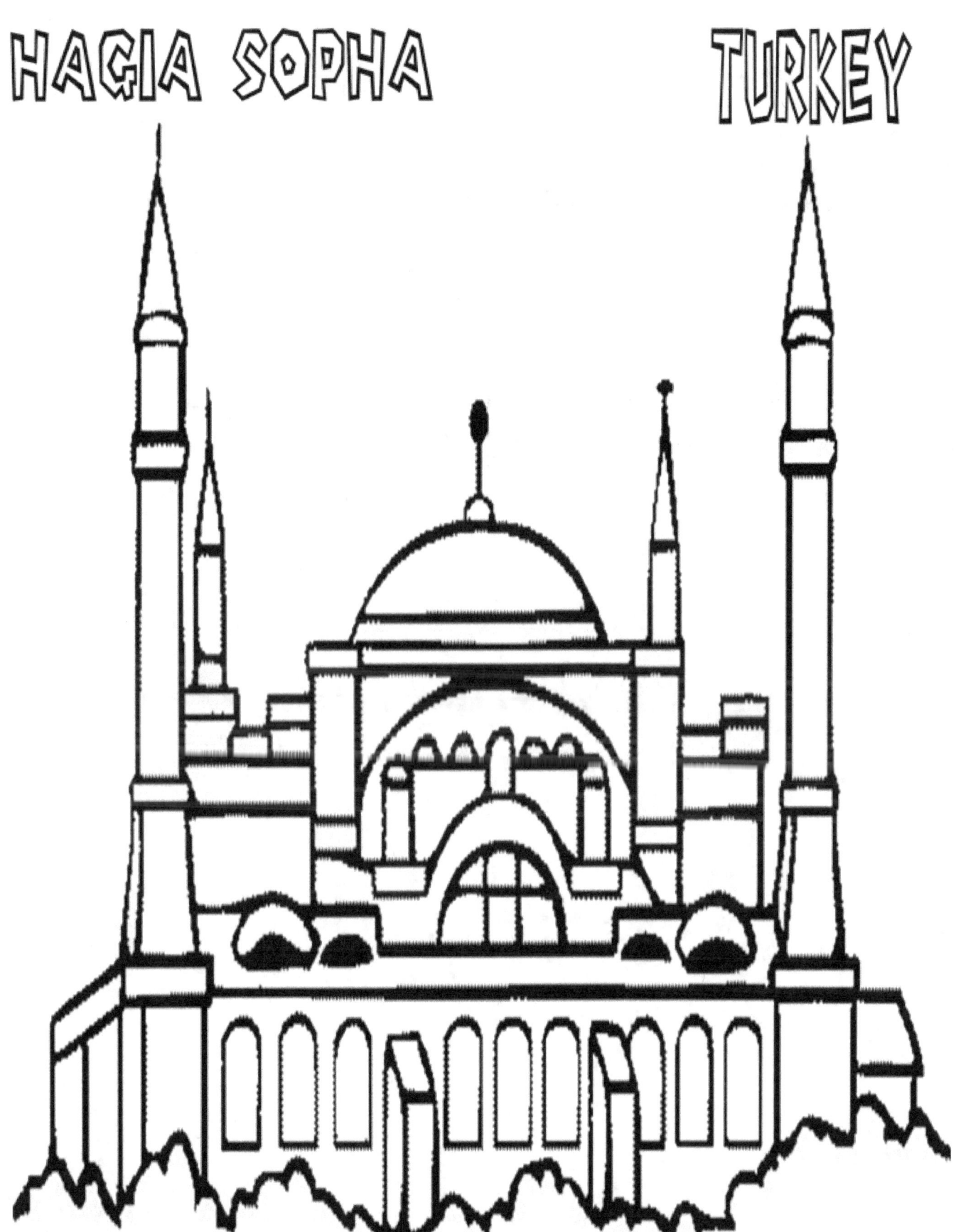

St. Basil's was built to commemorate the capture of the Tatar stronghold of Kazan in 1552, which occured on the Feast of the Intercession of the Virgin. The cathedral was thus officially named **Cathedral of the Intercession of the Virgin by the Moat**

The church is situation on Moscow's Red Square, and was bulit between 1555 and 1561

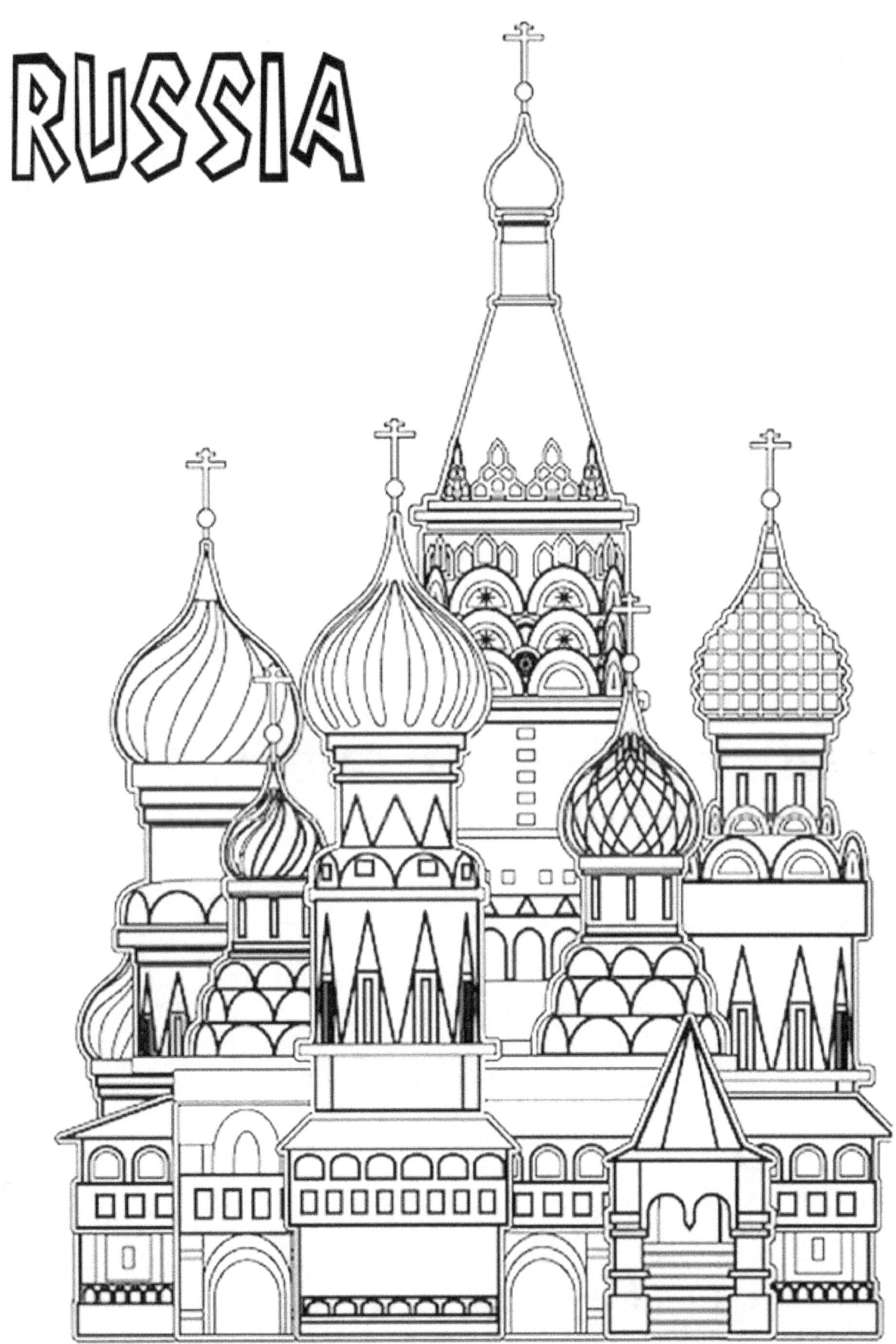

The **Sydney Opera House** is a multi-venue performing arts centre in Sydney, New South Wales, Australia. It is one of the 20th century's most famous and distinctive buildings

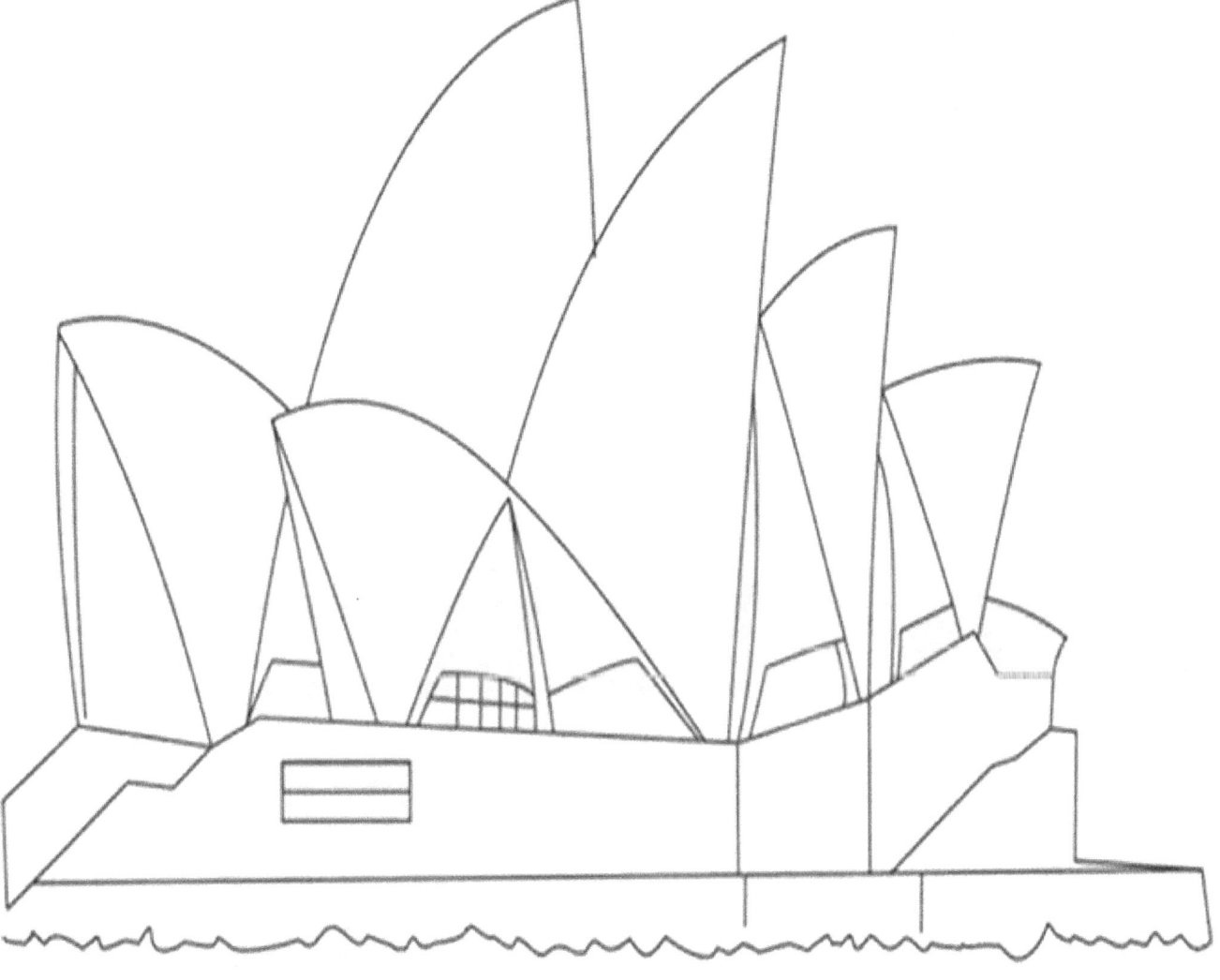

The Egyptian pyramids are ancient pyramid-shaped masonry structures located in Egypt.

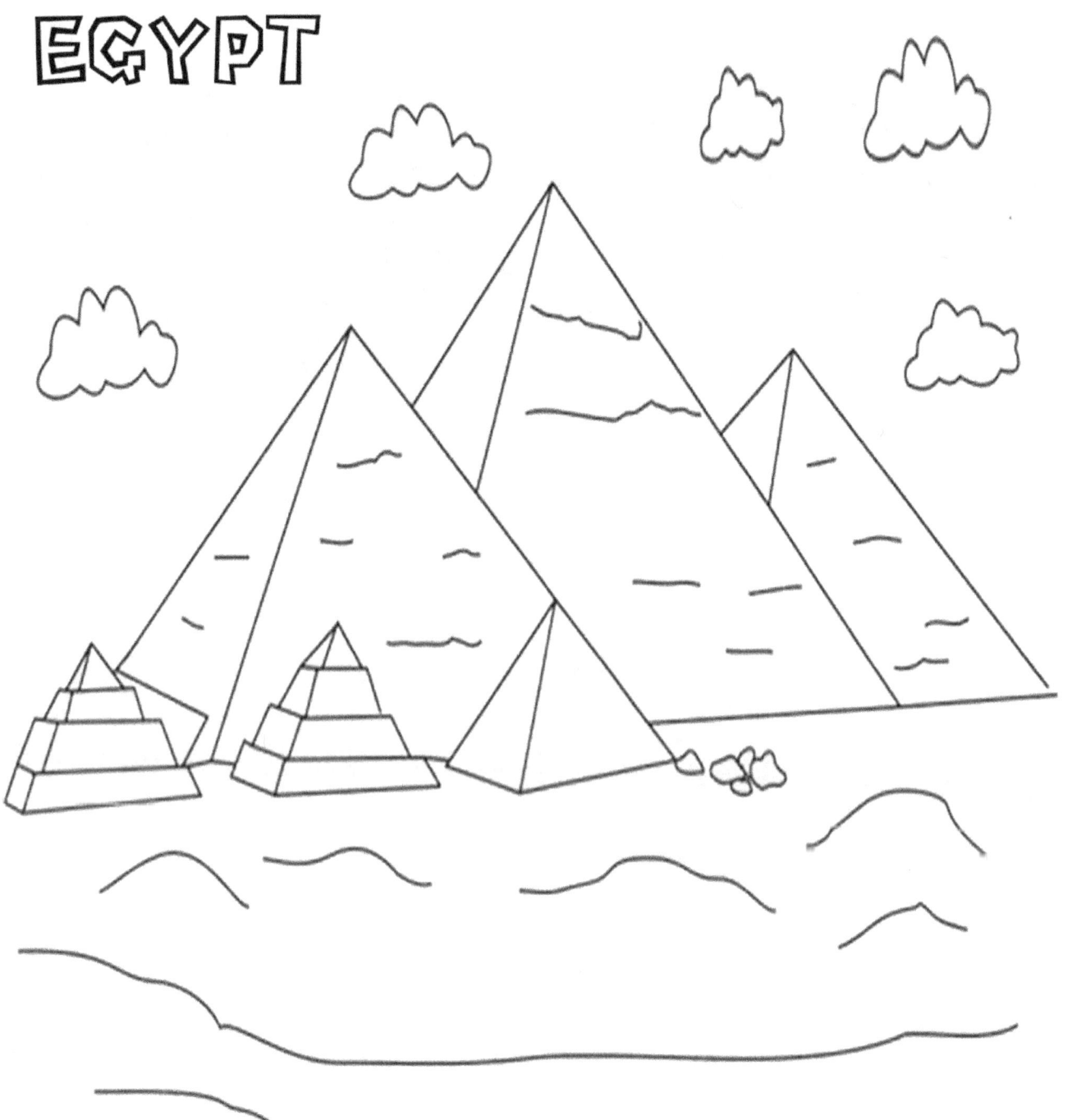

The word "sphinx", which means 'strangler', was first given by the Greeks to a fabulous creature which had the head of a woman, the body of a lion and the wings of a bird. In Egypt, there are numerous sphinxes, usually with the head of a king wearing his headdress and the body of a lion. There are, however, sphinxes with ram heads that are associated with the god Amun.

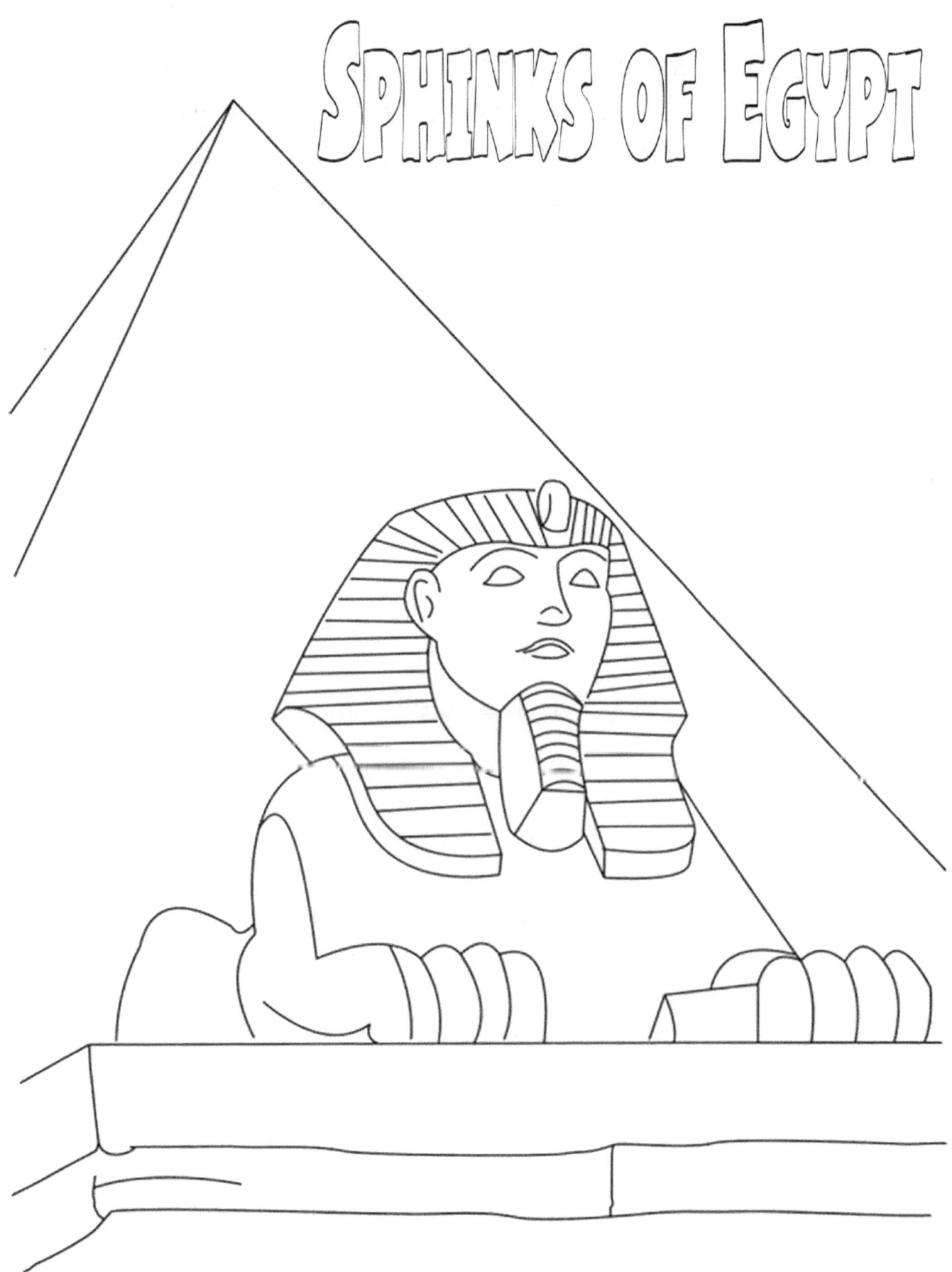

The Great Wall was not just a wall. It was an integrated military defensive system with watchtowers for surveillance, fortresses for command posts and logistics, beacon towers for communications, etc.

The Great Wall Of China

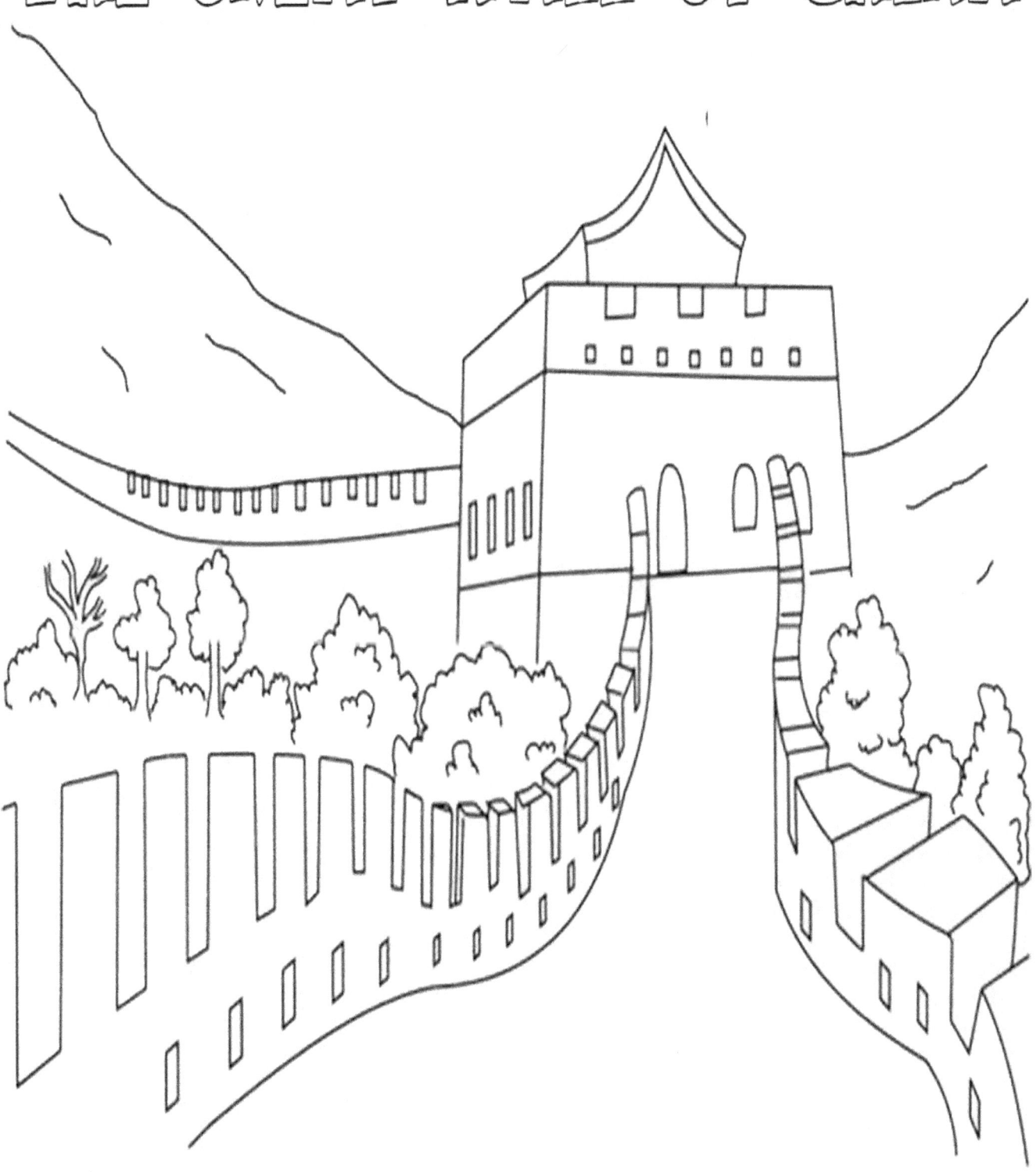

Osaka Castle is a Japanese castle in Chūō-ku, Osaka, Japan. The castle is one of Japan's most famous landmarks and it played a major role in the unification of Japan during the sixteenth century of the Azuchi-Momoyama period.]

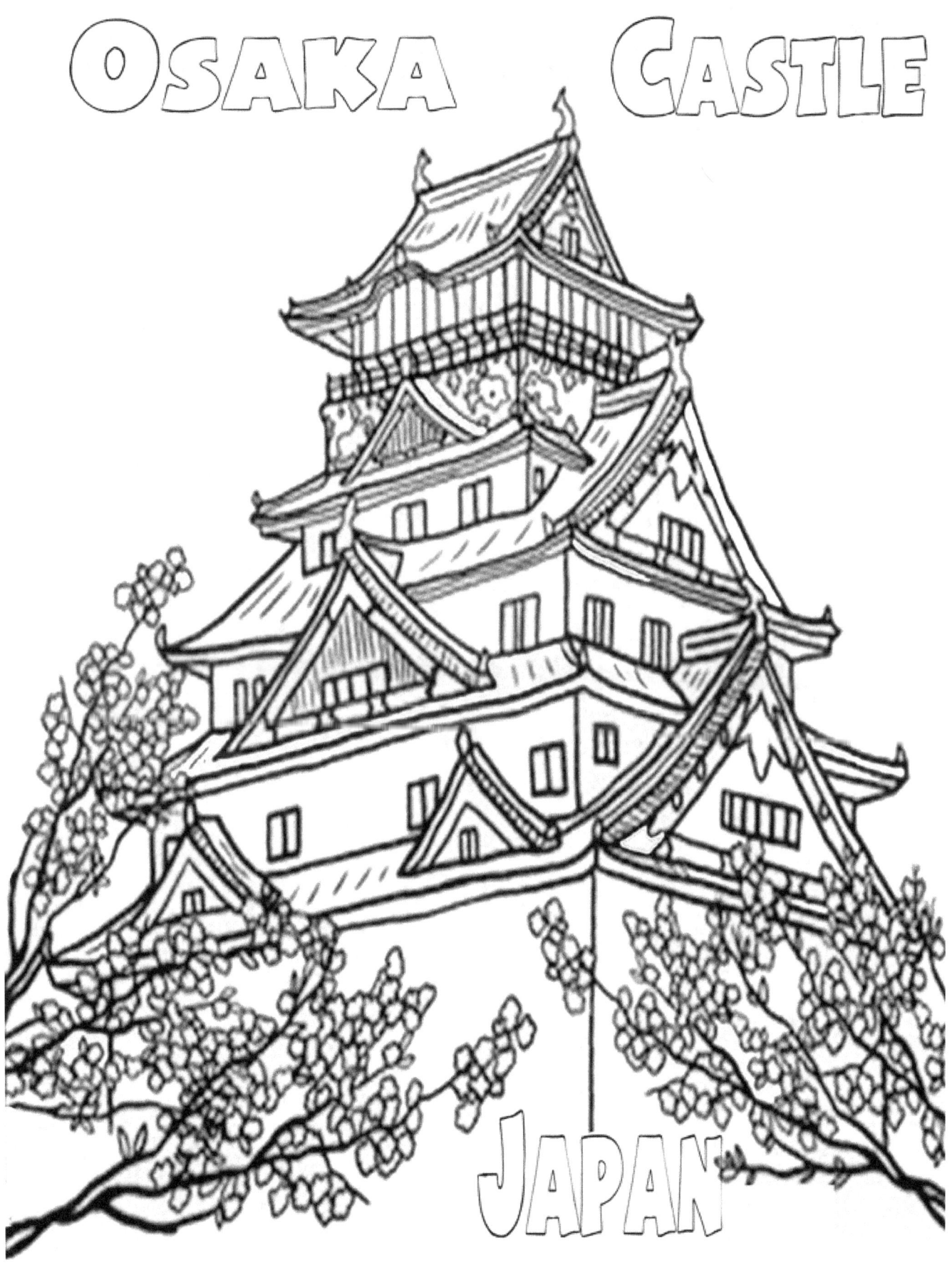

Tower of the Arabs is a luxury hotel located in Dubai, United Arab Emirates. It is the third tallest hotel in the world

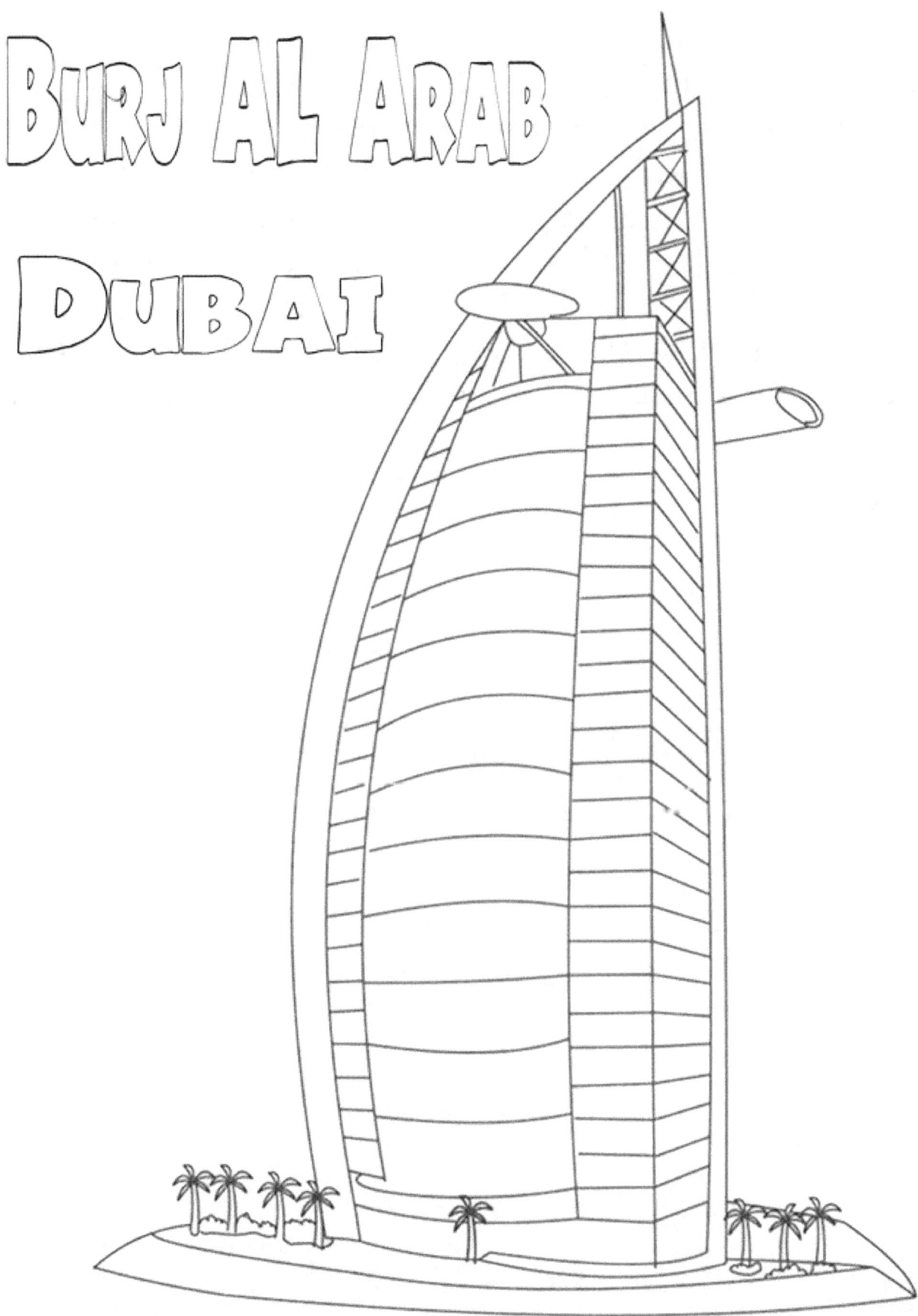

The Ka'aba (literally "the cube" in Arabic) is an ancient stone structure that was built and re-built by prophets as a house of monotheistic worship. It is located inside the Grand Mosque in Makkah (Mecca) Saudi Arabia. The Ka'aba is considered the center of the Muslim world, and is a unifying focal point for Islamic worship. When Muslims complete the Hajj pilgrimage to Makkah (Mecca), the ritual includes circling the Ka'aba.

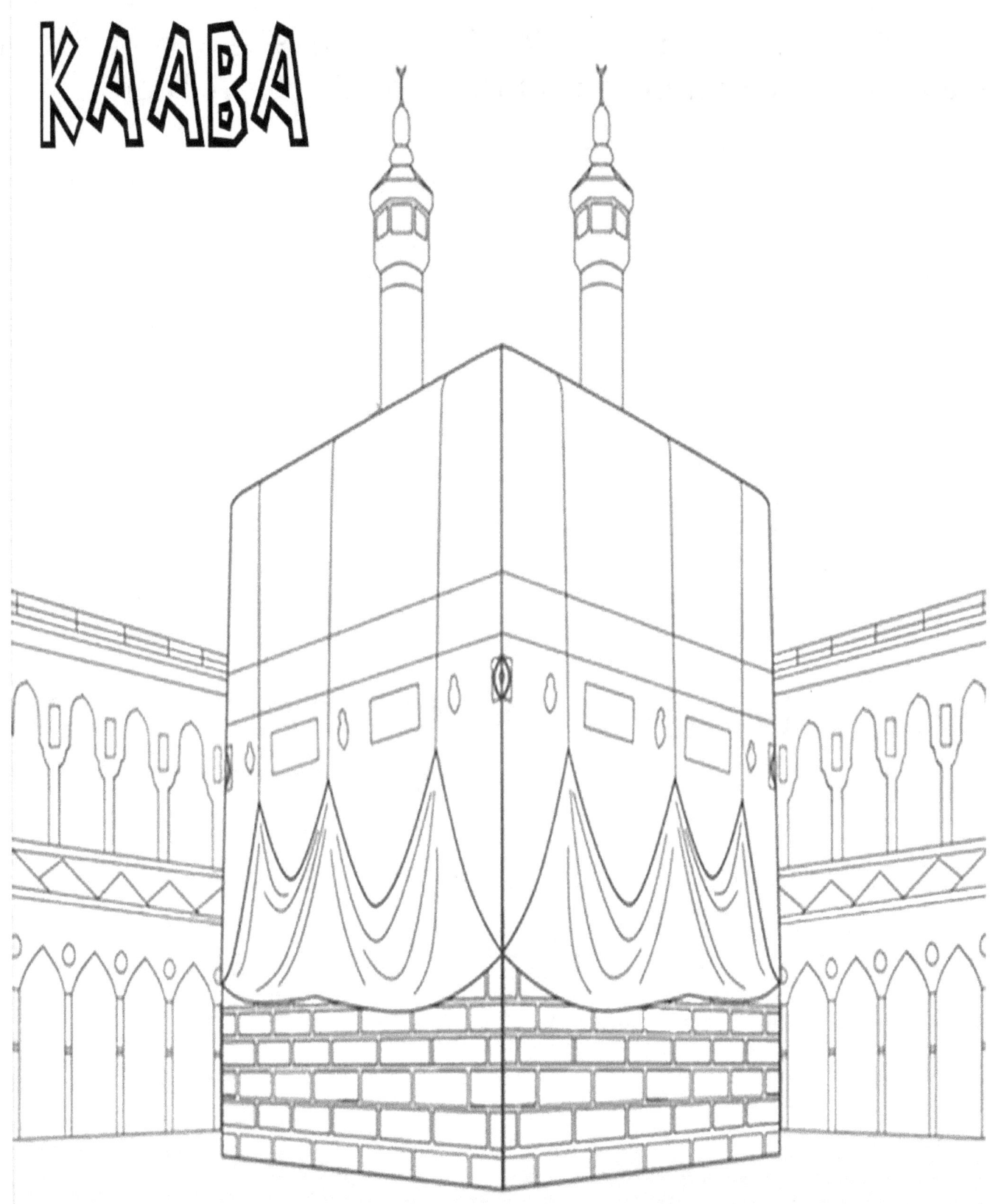

Hạ Long is a UNESCO World Heritage Site and popular travel destination in Quảng Ninh Province, Vietnam.

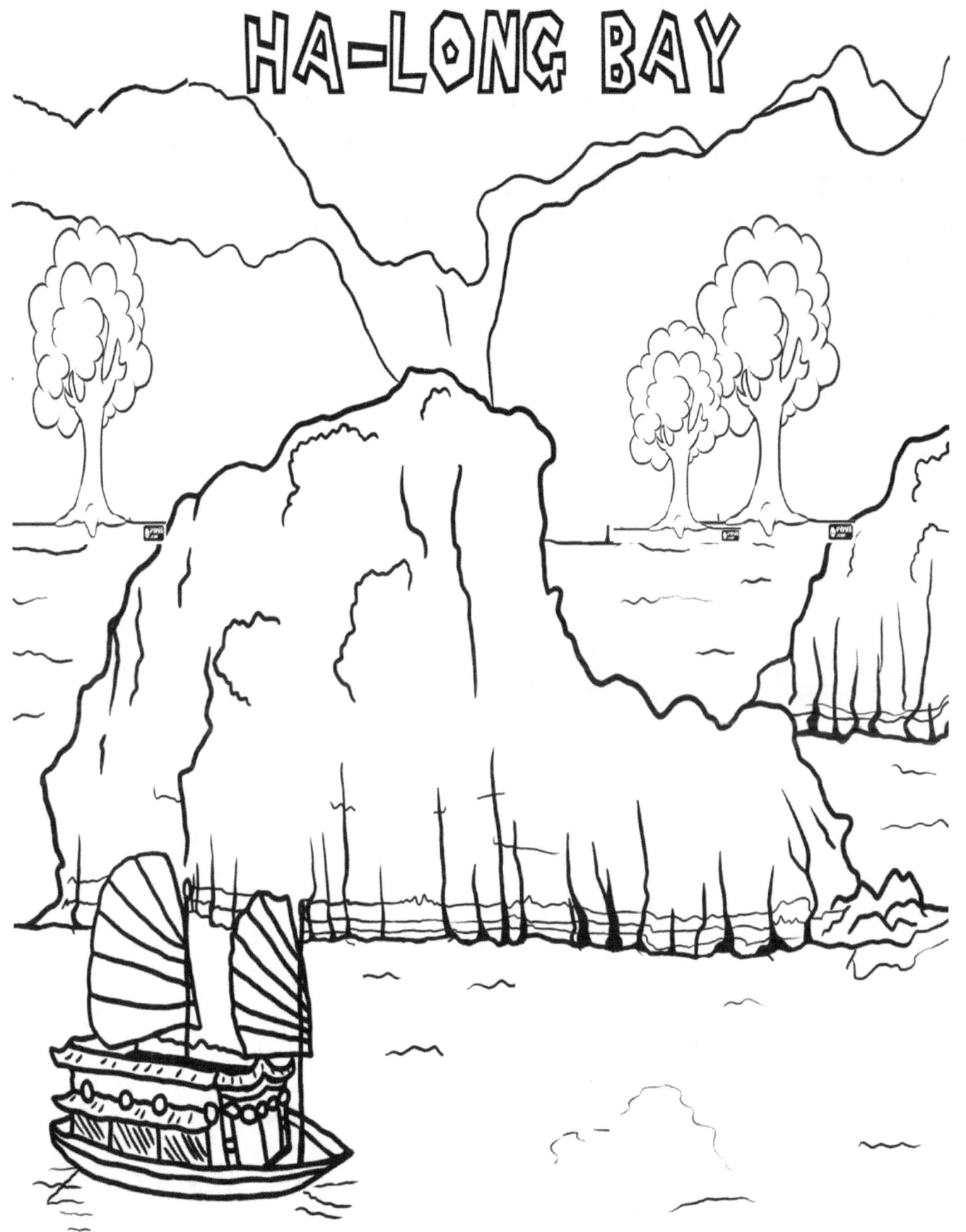

The Taj Mahal meaning Crown of the Palace is an ivory-white marble mausoleum on the south bank of the Yamuna river in the Indian city of Agra. It was commissioned in 1632 by the Mughal emperor, Shah Jahan (reigned 1628–1658), to house the tomb of his favourite wife

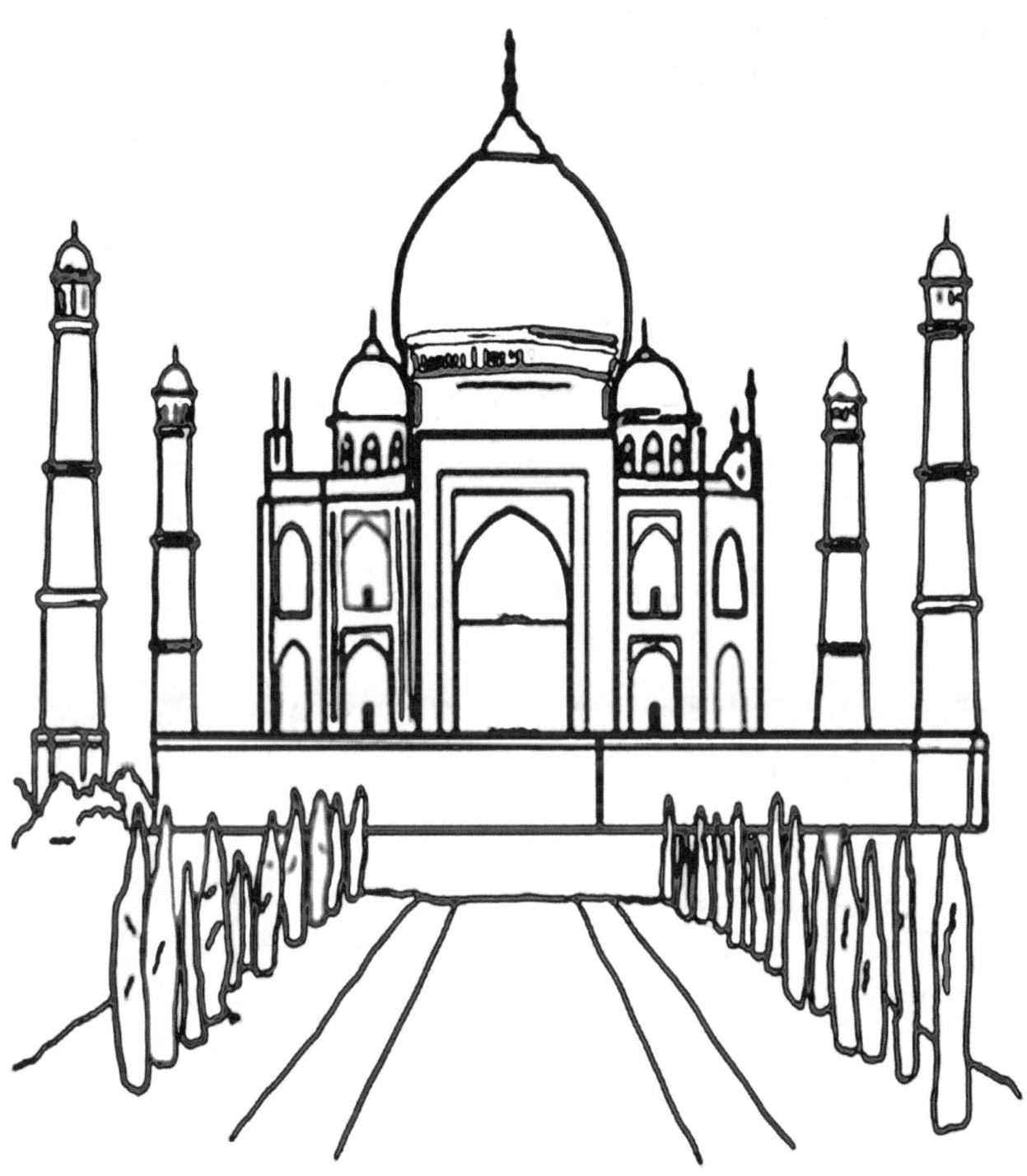

The Golden Gate Bridge is a suspension bridge spanning the Golden Gate, the one-mile-wide (1.6 km) strait connecting San Francisco Bay and the Pacific Ocean.

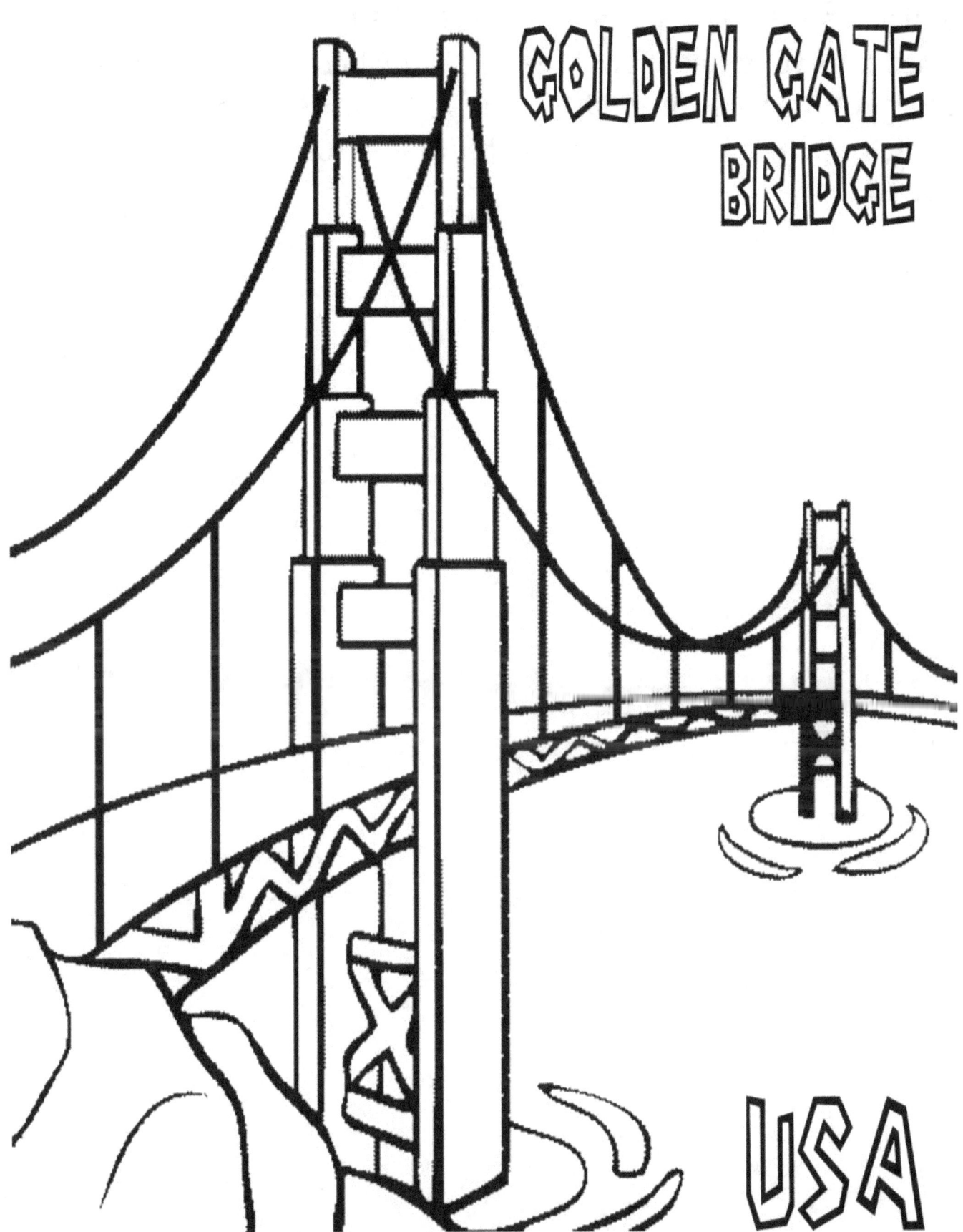

John F Kennedy Space Center

The first e manned NASA shuttle launched from Kennedy Space Center was in 1968. e crew of Apollo 8 were the -first human beings to exit Earth's orbit; travel round the Moon and back.

JOHN F. KENNEDY SPACE CENTER

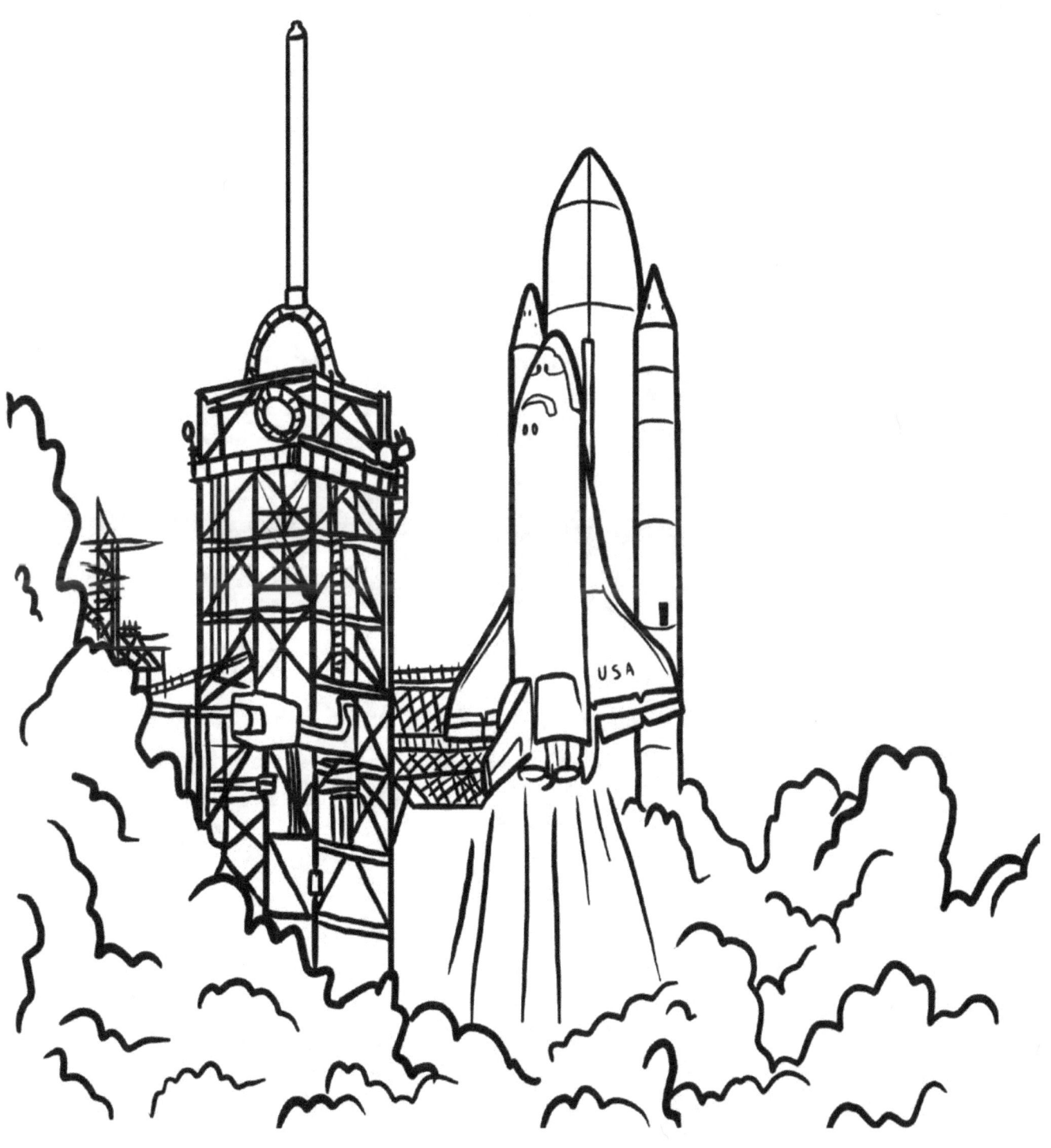

The **Gateway Arch** is a 630-foot (192 m) monument in St. Louis in the U.S. state of Missouri. Clad in stainless steel and built in the form of a weighted catenary arch,[5] it is the world's tallest arch,

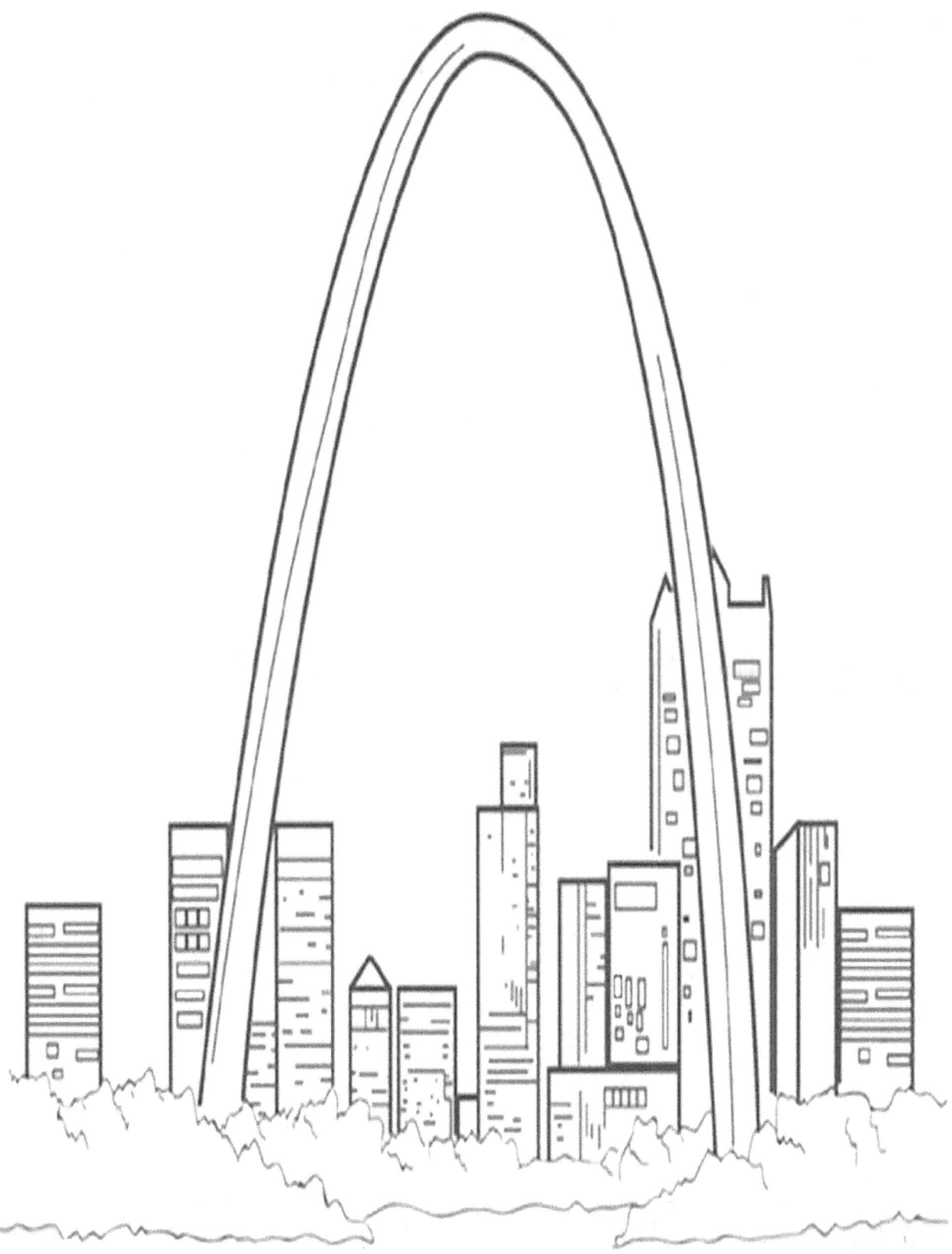

The **Statue of Liberty** is a colossal neoclassical sculpture on Liberty Island in New York Harbor in New York City, in the United States. The copper statue, a gift from the people of France to the people of the United States,

Statue of Liberty

USA

The **Empire State Building** is a Art Deco skyscraper on Fifth Avenue between West 33rd and 34th Streets in Midtown Manhattan, New York City. Designed by Shreve, Lamb & Harmon, the building has a roof height of 1,250 feet (380 m), and with its antenna included, it stands a total of 1,454 feet (443.2 m) tall. Its name is derived from "Empire State", the nickname for New York. As of 2017 the Empire State Building is the fifth-tallest completed skyscraper in the United States and the 28th-tallest in the world. It is also the sixth-tallest freestanding structure in the Americas. When measured by pinnacle height, it is the fifth-tallest building in the United States.

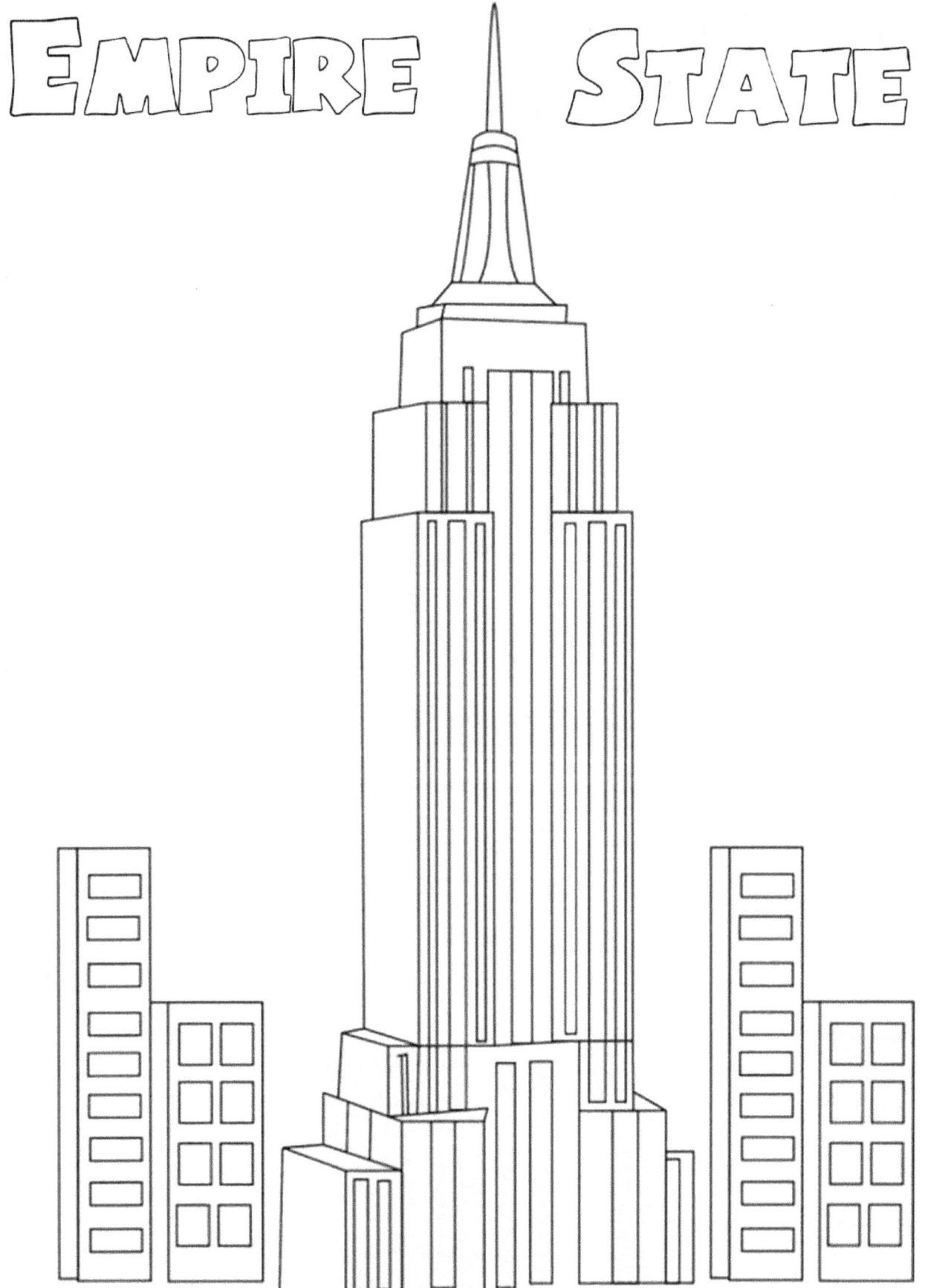

Niagara Falls is a city in Niagara County, New York, United States

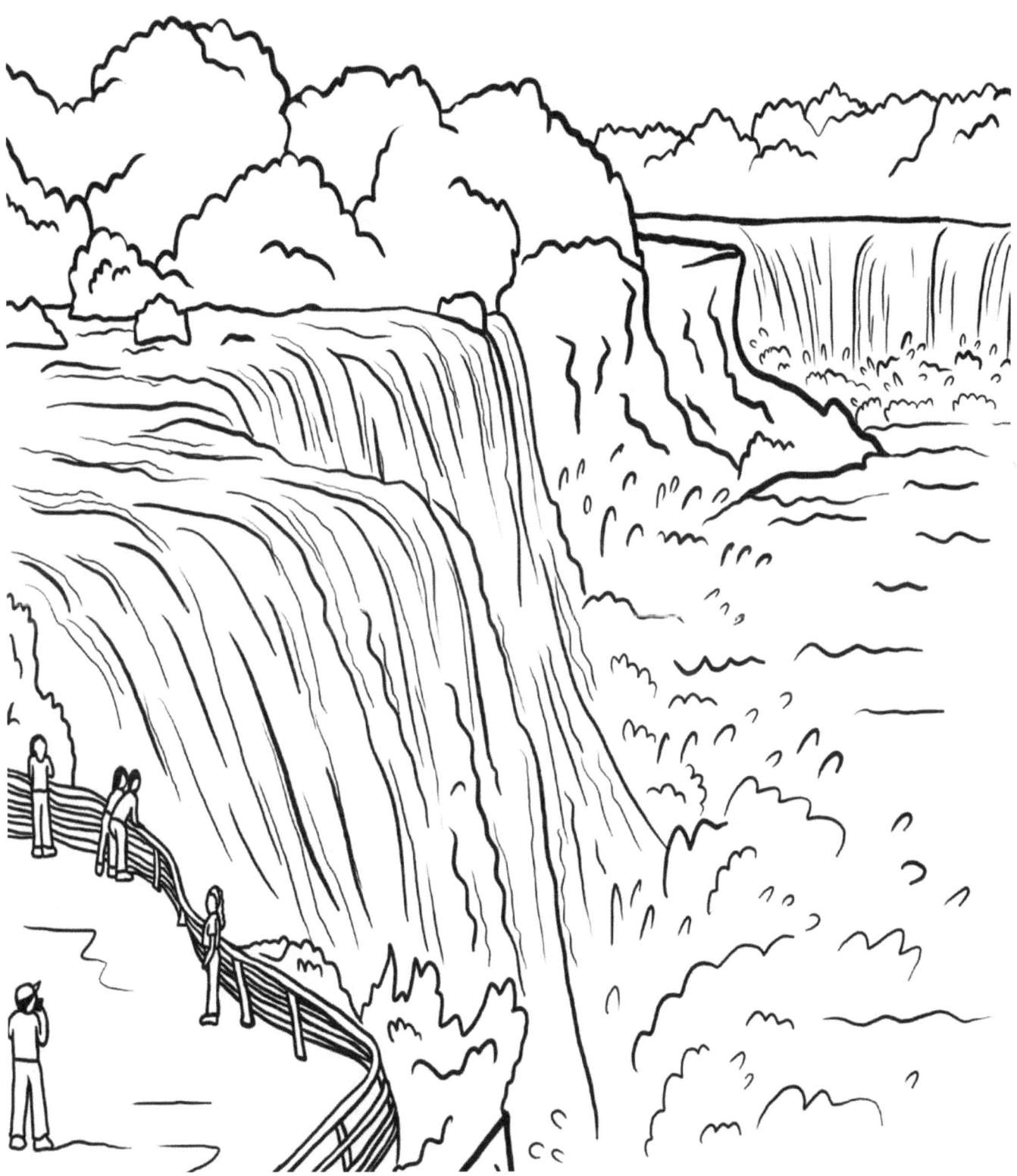

Christ the Redeemer is an Art Deco statue of Jesus Christ in Rio de Janeiro, Brazil,

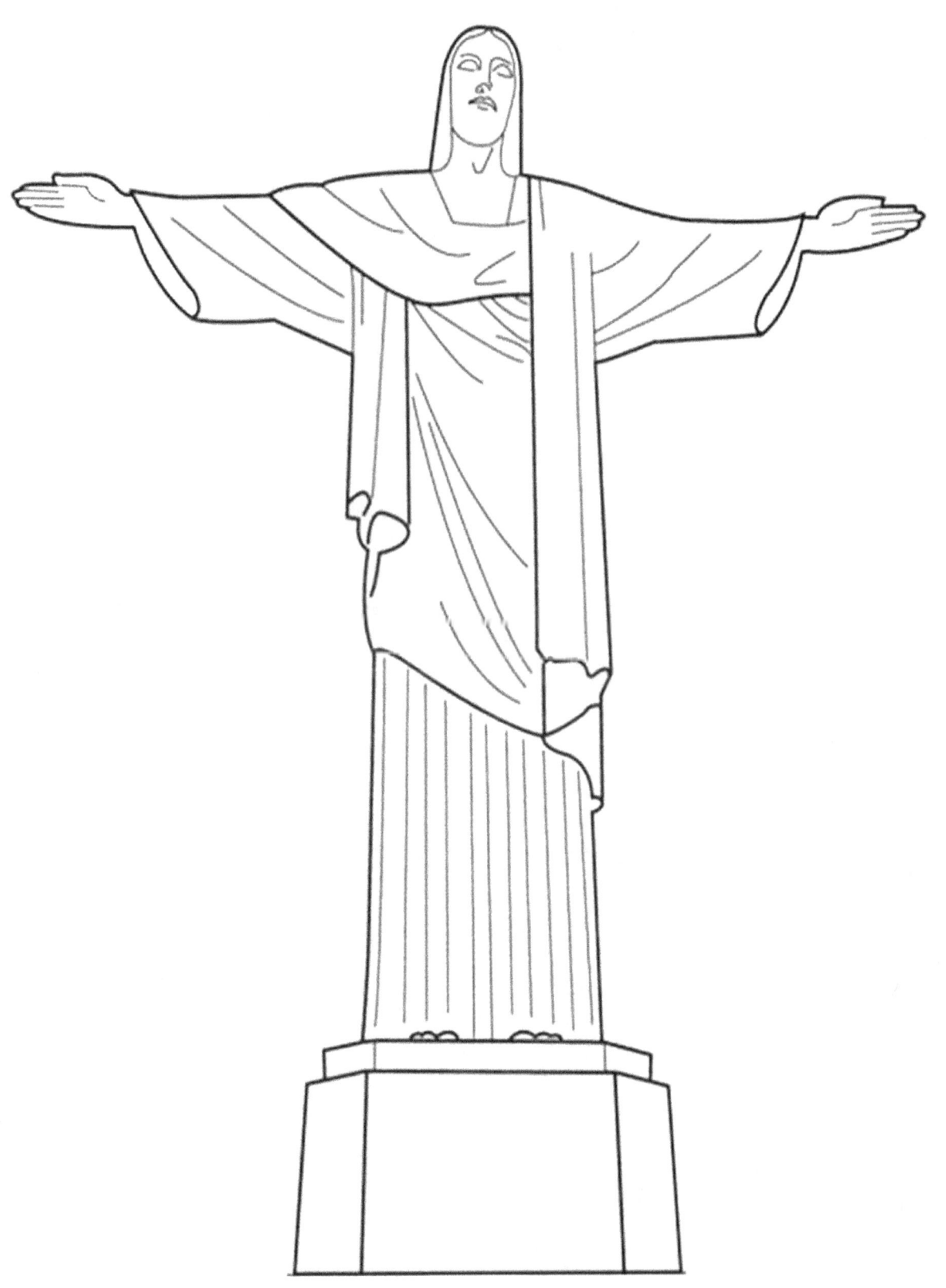

The **CN Tower** a 553.3 m-high (1,815.3 ft) concrete communications and observation tower in downtown Toronto, Ontario, Canada. Built on the former Railway Lands,

CN TOWER
TORONTO
CANADA

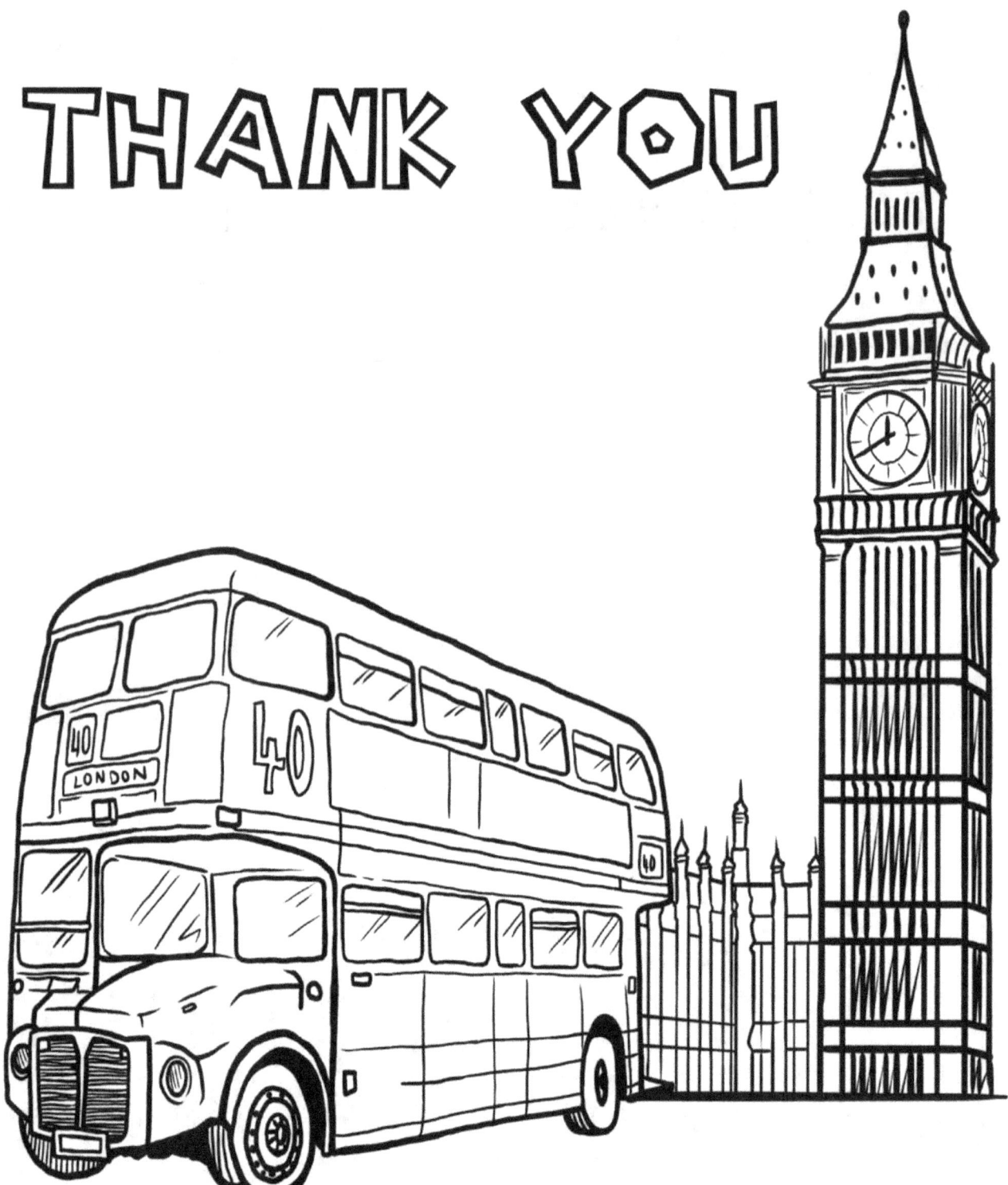

www.ingramcontent.com/pod-product-compliance
Lightning Source LLC
Chambersburg PA
CBHW082217220526
45470CB00010B/3208